Denise Goosby is a sweet soul whom [...]
the physical, emotional, and spiritua[...]
*Him* is a book that affords us the opportunity to peer into the life of
the author and mentally view a vivid picture of her scars. Through
the chronicling of her life's journey, Denise is able to see her scars as
a blessing from God. As you carefully read this book and reflect on
your own life, you may come to the realization that you too have been
scarred like Him. It may be therapeutic to meditate on the author's
script and biblical references and ask God to reveal His purpose for
your scars.

—Cinda Herring, pastor, Living Word Church in
Torrance, California

Denise's anointed and beautiful prose left me in tears. She is a modern-
day psalmist, a woman after God's own heart.

—Dr. Saundra Dalton-Smith, international speaker and
author of *Sacred Rest*

A stunning and profoundly uplifting testimony, *Scarred like Him* is
Denise Goosby's unflinching devotional declaration of what it means
to be "scarred" inside and out, yet redeemed by our Savior's healing,
beautiful love. Every page will encourage and empower! Five stars!

—Patricia Raybon, award-winning author of *My First White Friend,
I Told the Mountain to Move,* and *All That Is Secret*

# SCARRED LIKE HIM

# SCARRED LIKE HIM

*Seeing the Beauty in the Life You Live*

## DENISE ANN GOOSBY

Published by Redemption Press, PO Box 427, Enumclaw, WA 98022.
Toll-Free (844) 2REDEEM (273-3336)

Redemption Press is honored to present this title in partnership with the author. The views expressed or implied in this work are those of the author. Redemption Press provides our imprint seal representing design excellence, creative content, and high-quality production.

The author has tried to recreate events, locales, and conversations from memories of them. In order to maintain their anonymity, in some instances the names of individuals, some identifying characteristics, and some details may have been changed, such as physical properties, occupations, and places of residence.

ISBN 13: 978-1-64645-458-7 (Paperback)
978-1-64645-459-4 (ePub)
978-1-64645-460-0 (Mobi)

Library of Congress Catalog Card Number: 2021912212

# DEDICATION

My heart rejoices in the Eternal One;
my strength grows strong in the Eternal.
My mouth can mock my enemies
because I celebrate how You have saved me!

No one is holy like the Eternal One—
no one but You;
and there is no rock as solid as our True God.
Stop talking so proudly,
 and don't let such arrogance flow from your lips,
For the Eternal One is a True God who knows,
and He weighs the actions He sees.
The bows of the mighty crack in two,
but the feeble are given new strength.
Those who were full have had to work hard so they can eat,
but those who are starving have become fat with rich food.
The one who was infertile has borne seven children,
while the one who bore many sits alone in sadness.
The Eternal One kills and brings to life;
He sends down to the grave and raises up new life.
The Eternal One makes both poor and rich;
some He humbles and others He honors.
He lifts the poor up out of the dust, the needy from the trash heap.
He raises them to sit with princes and seats them on a glorious throne.
For the pillars of the earth are the Eternal One's,
and on them, He has set the world.

He will watch over the footsteps of the faithful,
but the wicked will be made silent in the darkness,
for one does not win by strength alone.
The Eternal One will shatter His foes;
from His throne in heaven, He will thunder with rage.
The Eternal One will be judge to the ends of the earth;
 He gives strength to His king,
And power to the one He chooses to rule. (1 Samuel 2:1–10 VOICE)

# CONTENTS

# FOREWORD

*Denise Goosby is a sweet* soul whom God has used to bring light to the physical, emotional, and spiritual scars of any reader. *Scarred Like Him* is a book that affords us the opportunity to peer into the life of the author and mentally view a vivid picture of her scars. Through the chronicling of her life's journey, Denise is able to see her scars as a blessing from God. As you carefully read this book and reflect on your own life, you may come to the realization that you, too, have been scarred like Him. While the pages are few, it may be therapeutic to meditate on the author's script and biblical references and ask God to reveal His purpose for your scars.

—Pastor Cinda Herring of Living Word Church, Torrance, California

# ACKNOWLEDGMENTS

*Because you are special to Me and I love you, I gladly give up other peoples for you;*
*. . . They are trivial by comparison to your weighty significance.*
Isaiah 43:4 VOICE

*I have heard it said* that our days are long but our years are short. And every one of them has been made invaluable and worthwhile because of the God I serve. I am thankful for the many people He has sent my way who have made my life and writing journey richer, kinder, and more Christ centered.

Thank you, Daddy, for faithfully loving me with all your heart and for leaving me an eternal legacy of faith in Jesus. I love you both because you first loved me.

Thank you to my mom, aunts, and other family members who watched over me and encouraged me.

To all my teachers who encouraged my love of writing—Mrs. Coulter, Mrs. Patterson, Mrs. Hornbein, Miss Myers, Sister Leona, Sister Joseph Ellen, Father O'Brien, Dr. Brueck, and so many others who inspired me to express myself in words—I offer you and your families my gratitude and blessing.

Thank you to the faculty, staff, students, and parents of Nevin Avenue Elementary School in Los Angeles for teaching me to be a better educator and person. Thank you to those I met there who pointed me to Jesus.

Thank you to the Ingersoll family and all the faculty, staff, students, and parents of Pines Christian School in Harbor City for showing me such love, kindness, and friendship. You continue to encourage and bless me in so many ways.

Thank you so much to Leila, Troy, Pat, Dianne, Maria, Mendy, and Pastor Cliff for your love and friendship. Praise God for those who stick closer than a brother.

Thank you to my mentor Professor Helen Mitchell, Kayley Allen, and all my instructors and counselors at Biola University for guiding me, inspiring me, comforting me, and showing me that I was not too old to start over.

Great appreciation to Angela Collins, who handles my website, and Shameka McCoy, who has helped with the promotion of this book. God truly sent you lovely ones just for me. You are awesome!

This book would not have been written without all that I learned from Hope Writers, Flourish Writers, Speak Up, West Coast Christian Writers, and She Writes for Him. Thank you, Leslie Fields, for your wonderful book that showed me how to write my story. My Hope Circle writer friends—Valerie, Katie, Linsey, Jennifer, and Robyn—you are such a blessing to me. I am so proud of all of you. Keep writing for God's glory.

Praise God for my Abide small group of Saddleback South Bay. You embraced me as a new member and literally prayed me through most of the writing of this book. It is amazing how God knows who to bring into your life at just the right moment. Laurie, Miriam, Kathy, Linda, Melinda, Melissa, Ronnie, Albi, Linda, Shona, and Pratima, I wish you love and prayers.

And to Athena, Jennifer E., Dori, Cynthia, Hannah, Micah, Stephanie, Dr. Dalton-Smith, Tammy, Jennifer and all the tremendous people at Redemption Press, thank you for believing in me and my story. Yes, truly, God has sent you for my life, and I am so grateful.

—Denise Ann Goosby

# INTRODUCTION

*The Lord has appeared of old to me, saying: "Yes, I have loved you with an everlasting love; Therefore with lovingkindness I have drawn you."*
Jeremiah 31:3 NKJV

*Everyone wants to be loved.*
Everyone wants to be accepted.
Everyone wants to be desired.

But what happens when that longing eludes you? What happens when the physical, mental, emotional, and spiritual scars of living mark you as different? Someone who others feel may not deserve love, acceptance, and desire?

What happens when you don't fit society's vision for what is beautiful—or your own?

*Scarred Like Him: Seeing the Beauty in the Life You Live* tells a story of how our outer and inner wounds affect our identity, worth, and value in the eyes of others . . . and in the eyes of ourselves.

Most importantly, *Scarred Like Him* shows us the power we have when we replace lies with truth. It shows the triumph we experience when we replace the often false, limiting, and negative beliefs we have about ourselves with God's redemptive, grace-filled, and truthful view of our beauty.

Scars mark us all. No one on this earth escapes being wounded. Your scars may have come from others, or they may have been self-inflicted. They may have occurred on the battlefield or on the schoolyard. Maybe you got them in a boardroom or even at a church potluck. Scars can afflict our minds, bodies, souls, and spirits. They trick us into believing there is no beauty in them or in our lives.

Whether visible or invisible, we carry scars and too often view ourselves in light of them. Our scars are ugly, so we see ourselves as ugly. We don't want anyone touching them, so we see ourselves as untouchable. They show we are flawed, so we see ourselves as flawed, less than, or unworthy. They may fade, but they never go away—on display for the world to see. We need healing, but our lives seem beyond redemption. And we are terrified others will see us that way too.

But our inner and outer afflictions—our scars—tell the truth of God's faithfulness and workings in us and through us. Where there are scars, there is healing. They show that God has kept us. That we are alive. That we endure. The pain of living in this world has not broken us. We must remember we are the offspring of a beautiful God.

Yes, honey, you are beautiful.

You are beautiful, though that's not the most important point. Know that you are already loved, accepted, and desired. You are not defined by your looks. Your failures do not have the final say. Your afflictions may weary you, but they will not overcome you.

You and I do not have to hide in shame because of our scars.

The God who sings over us in delight (Zephaniah 3:17) is not put off by our scars. The One who lovingly and sacrificially bares His own scars is willing and able to comfort and strengthen us, anointing our scars to bless others and bring honor to Him.

Dear one, like you, I am scarred like Him. I am very well acquainted with scars and have been for a long, long time. I've learned a lot about myself and God because of my scars, and I want to share all of it with you.

For more than forty years, I've daily endured the pain, suffering, and disfigurement of severe keloid scarring. According to Harvard University Health, "keloids are raised overgrowths of scar tissue that occurs at the site of a skin injury."[1] If someone asks me about my keloids, I say I have sensitive skin that over heals when wounded—essentially too much healing.

Keloids can also arise when no visible trauma has occurred. They usually appear on the upper body—on the chest, back, shoulders, and face. The condition is not wellknown, yet millions of people struggle with keloids. Both men and women get them. They tend to appear during one's preteen or young adult years.[2] It is estimated that some eleven million people worldwide suffer from keloids. Healthline.com documents that some 10 percent of the population suffer from keloids. Like me, many of those afflicted with keloids are African American and other people of color.[3]

My scars are not just inconvenient. My physical scars can dictate how I spend my days and nights. They are on my back, chest, left shoulder, and stomach. A long thin one stretches from my ear to my chin on my left cheek. They hurt. They itch. They get infected. They rob me of my sleep and energy. They wreak havoc with my thoughts and emotions. They can make me feel depressed and lonely. And sometimes they even stir up my anger toward God.

Often I wish I were never born. My scars isolate me. I fear to have people touch me or even get close to me. What if they pull back? What if my scars are too much for them to handle? What if I am too much to handle? The emotional damage is almost more painful than the physical.

Have you felt that way too?

Not all our scars are physical. We have all heard, seen, and experienced things.

My friend, I want something better for me—and for you. Aren't you tired of what ifs? I am. I want to see the wonder God has put in me

---

1 "Keloids," Harvard Health Publishing, Harvard Medical School, April 2019, https://www.health.harvard.edu/.

2 Rachel Nall, "Everything You Need to Know About Keloid Scars," medically reviewed by Cynthia Cobb, Healthline.com.

3 "Bone," https://www.merriam-webster.com/.

and in you. I want to live by the truth of who I am in Christ. Instead of fearing that people will reject me, I want to bask in God's acceptance. I want to see with the eyes of my heart—the spiritual eyes that God gave me—the beauty in the life He has given me to live.

I want the same for you too. I want us to continue to learn how to value ourselves and live serving God and others. I want us to be encouraged, validated, motivated, and inspired to be our own unique, beautiful selves. This is the truth of who we are. But it is a battle to believe the truth—a battle that encompasses our entire lives. We are not fighting to believe a lie. We are fighting to believe the truth. We are worth the fight.

*Scarred Like Him* is a journey of discovery that uses story, music, devotions, and Scripture to free us from the hurtful lies that life often teaches, enabling us to receive the truth of God's love, favor, and acceptance. Through testimony, worship, and God's Word, we can know true healing.

I only ask one thing of you: come as you are.

If you have sorrow, let the tears fall. If you are skeptical, bring your doubts. If you fear the pain of your scars is too much, do it afraid. The Jesus who beckoned Thomas to touch His scars will give you the courage to touch your own. Through the words, songs, and readings in this book, I pray for God to meet you where you are. Take the journey and discover a healing that can only come when we offer up our most vulnerable selves to the One who sees all that we are, all that we can be, all that is beautiful—in Him.

Would you join me?

*Father God, I thank You for this beautiful soul You led to pick up this book.* Father, please bless and keep them. Please speak to them through these words and songs. Give them eyes to see You. Let them know that You see them. You see their pain. You hear their prayers. And You see the beauty that lies within them. Father God, love them with Your everlasting love and show Yourself mighty on their behalf. Amen.

# Chapter 1

# WHO AM I?

*From now on, don't let anyone trouble me with these things. For I bear on my body the scars that show I belong to Jesus.*
Galatians 6:17 NLT

*I shuffled into the bathroom,* anxious to get the day started but unsure if I had the energy required to live it. I hadn't slept the best last night. Again. No matter how many times I turned, I couldn't get to sleep. But I was thankful. Somewhere after 2:00 or 3:00 a.m., my body gave up the fight and I drifted off to sleep.

I made it through another night.

*Thank you, Lord.* I rose from my couch. *Thank You for giving me sleep.* I folded the blankets somewhat neatly and left them on my couch.

Thank God for that couch.

An anxious breath escaped me. Every night I fight to sleep. I constantly fear I will never get enough. I hadn't slept in my bed for weeks, and the last time I did, it was only for a few hours. Since I bought it nearly three years ago, I doubt if I had spent more than a month of sleep time in it. The only time I felt comfortable in it was the first week I moved to the apartment after selling my house—after my dad had died and I fell into it grieving and exhausted.

Determined now to get the day started, I pushed back the shower curtain and carefully stepped into the tub. A song came to me: "The

Goodness of God," by Jenn Johnson of Bethel. It talks about loving God for being a good Father who stays close—a God who delivers you in and through the fire. As I sung the lovely words under the warmth of the gentle spray, I felt a familiar sensation in my chest. It was part pressure, part pain. I looked down to see a drop of blood fall, followed by another. And another. I continued to sing. "Through the fire. . ."

For me, that fire began in my childhood when both my outer and inner scars formed and where self-doubt, fear, and others' choices combined to answer the question for me: "Who am I?"

I remembered back to one of those sunny, blue-sky California days that the Beach Boys made famous in their surfer songs back in the day. I remember standing on the sidewalk by the white iron fence that separated my family's yard from my mom's relatives next door. My eight-year-old mind drank in my surroundings, not wanting to miss a thing. My head turned in the direction of laughter coming from two or three preteen boys who talked and hit each other and messed around, as boys will do out of sight of grownups. I watched them for a few moments. Their fun attracted me, but I figured they didn't want a little girl interrupting their horseplay.

They turned and looked at me, continuing to laugh and joke around. But now their focus was on me. That's when I saw the dog. It might have been a collie or a young German shepherd. I vaguely remember it being mostly white with black splotches on its body.

One of the boys said something to me. I looked at the ground and shuffled my feet on the concrete. I didn't know the boys. Maybe they were friends of my cousins. I raised my head and looked at them steadily, trying to be brave.

I knew what it was like to be teased and bullied. My brown, chubby body and pigtails made an attractive target. In my neighborhood, there was an older teenage boy who often frightened me. Sometimes he would approach when I walked on my street. He would come close to my face and threaten me. He said I was fat and he didn't like me, and it seemed that my very existence offended him.

Sometimes school kids would kick the backs of my legs on the playground. They ran away as they looked at me and laughed. One boy called me "nigger." Outraged, I ran to a teacher nearby and told her what he said to me.

"That's supposed to be a bad word?" the teacher questioned.

"Yes," I said, bewildered. Blinking, I backed up, my eyes searching her face. Everyone knew that word was bad. How could she—a Black woman—not know how awful that word was?

Seemingly amused, the teacher asked him, "Did you call her a nigger?"

The boy, who was darker than me, looked at her, then dropped his gaze. It hurt to hear the mirth in her voice. She smiled as she spoke to him. I watched them. After a few moments, she turned and walked away. Relieved, the little boy walked in the opposite direction. I looked at him, speechless, then went back to my own play, disappointed that the teacher chose not to punish the boy for calling me that word. Why wouldn't this teacher stick up for me? Why wouldn't she defend me?

The dog yelped. One of the boys held the dog's upper body. Then the dog flew. I could see the fear in the dog's eyes. But before I could react, the dog's face hit me in my chest. I don't think it meant to attack me, but its startled cry turned into an angry growl as its teeth scratched my upper chest a few inches from my heart. A small scratch with reddish, broken skin appeared.

Somehow the dog's bite went no deeper. Somehow I did not fall and become even more vulnerable to the dog or the boys' malicious game. I stumbled backward and kept moving. I was afraid the dog would attack me in earnest. Mercifully, a boy grabbed the dog, and I quickly left.

To my knowledge, I never saw those boys or that dog again. I never knew why they pushed the dog at me or what their ultimate intentions were. In a few seconds, the incident was over, and we all moved on. Yet I would never be the same. Soon after the attack, small lumps of raised skin started appearing on my chest. They didn't hurt or itch, but they remained, slowly multiplying throughout my childhood.

My inner scars grew, too, and became my teachers. They helped to define my identity. They taught me I was lacking, that something was wrong with me, that I took up too much space. People saw me as not beautiful—not worthy of their friendship and protection. To me it was clear—people would hurt me. I needed to do everything I could to keep them from hurting me. I needed to please them. I needed to make myself valuable to them. And if I failed to make myself acceptable, then I withdrew from people and created my own inner world where I was beautiful and strong and loved.

It never occurred to me that God thought differently about me than others did. I thought my existence offended Him too. I remember feeling afraid of God as a girl. The things of the divine shook me. My first memory as a toddler is of having some huge, otherworldly thing come at me while I sat alone on the couch crying, terrified, and alone. Maybe I equated God to whatever threatened me in that living room. Maybe I saw Him as this big, scary thing I had to somehow please and placate so He would not hurt me. I just knew I feared Him—feared what He could do to me.

But now, God is the God I sing to in my middle age. The words of the song poured through me as a prayer. The God I feared as a child has "led me through the fire." He guides me and orders my steps. He comforts me. He forgives me, even when I feel angry at Him. In Him, I know who I am. I know who He is. And He gives me all I need.

The Lord is my shepherd, I lack nothing. (Psalm 23:1)

Our scars speak to us in loud, obnoxious voices. Our experiences are real. Our struggles are real. Our pain and suffering are real. But we do not give up. We push through the hurt and grab onto God's Word because it tells us the truth of who we are. It says we are God's beloved offspring, handmade by our loving Father. It says this Father chose and adopted us and sees our value and beauty. Our perfect Father sent His perfect Son, Jesus, to live, bleed, and die, scarred to bring us to Him forever. God does not reject us or deem us unworthy. He is not put off by our scars—instead He lovingly touches them and embraces us. God will never let us go.

> I have called you by name: you are mine. When you pass through the waters, I will be with you; and through the rivers, they shall not overwhelm you; when you walk through the fire you shall not be burned, and the flame shall not consume you. For I am the LORD your God, the Holy One of Israel, your Savior. (Isaiah 43:1–3 ESV)

Life will continue to assault us. Things will happen. People will hurt us. We will make bad decisions and forget who we are. This has been my story. Is it yours? Feel encouraged despite the hard road you may be on. You do not walk it alone. Travel with me a little longer. I want to show you how faithful God can be. This God who bathes our scars in love and grace is the One who never gives up on us—who never gives up on you.

## "You're Worth It to Me"
By Denise Ann Goosby

The future is a whirlwind of darkness.
Fear and triumph battle within.
A lifetime of hopes and promises
Still waiting to be lived,
Even as twilight appears—

Am I worth the effort?
Am I worth being with?
Knowing that destiny awaits . . . and He's good.

Leaning on me or leaning on You?
Too old for dreams,
Who am I to become?
Is waiting all I'll ever do?
Will promise and potential die with me?

As my flesh and my heart fail,
Oh, God, I turn trembling to You.

The God Who sees, the God Who understands
I haven't been this way before.
You say, Believe I'm good.
Believe I'm enough.
Believe I'm in love with you.
And be okay with that.
You're worth it to Me.

I'm not afraid of your doubts.
I'm not afraid of your fears.
Your scars are precious to Me.
Your battles have become My own—
Know that I will never leave.

Your God does all things well,
Including loving you.
Even in your trembling, trust Me—
I'm making your life beautifully new.

I'm the God Who sees, the God Who understands,
And I know you haven't been this way before.

Just . . . believe that I'm good,
And believe I'm enough,
Believe . . . that I'm in love with you . . .
And be okay with that.

Believe I'm good.
Believe I'm enough.
Believe I'm in love with you . . .
Believe you're worth it to Me.

Let My blood and My scars prove to you
You're worth it to Me.

© Denise Ann Goosby 2020

### Devotion

### When I Look in the Mirror

*God saw all that he had made, and it was very good. And there was*
*evening, and there was morning—the sixth day.*
Genesis 1:31

Sometimes it is hard to fathom that God took His time in making me
and that I am good in His eyes. When I look in the mirror—something
I am often loathe to do—and when I consider the disappointments of
life, good is not what I see. Flawed is what I see. Lacking is what I see.
Struggle is what I see. My own sin is what I see. And I cringe.

How easy it is for the Enemy disguised as other hurting and
broken people—even, sadly, as my own inner voice—to play upon
my doubts, fears, and losses and to suggest that I am not who God
says I am . . . good.

Yet God is my defender, and He is yours too. He knows our experiences and our circumstances and how the evil in this world tries to
lure us away from His truth. So God pursues us. He speaks to us in our
pain and suffering, offering us comfort. He sends His word through
His messengers or the Bible, and He heals us. God woos us through
promises, which He takes great delight in fulfilling. Even in the dark
times, He gives us hidden treasures of hope and grace. He provides
strength to match our days. We are good because God, who is infinitely
good, says we are.

Our words, actions, motivations, and thoughts are not always
good, but God gives us grace. His forgiveness and kindness turns us
back to Him. We can rest in this.

**Questions to Ponder in Your Heart**

What do I see when I look in the mirror?

Who am I in my own eyes? Who do I want to be?

How does God see me?

**Prayer**

*Heavenly Father, You have pronounced me good.* When I look in the mirror, help me see the beauty You placed in me. Let me live in freedom and peace knowing that despite all that has happened to me, You, by Your Spirit, are working beauty and goodness in my life. In Your name I pray, Amen.

**Memory Verse**

> But to all who believed him and accepted him, he gave the right to become children of God. (John 1:12 NLT)

# Chapter 2

# WHY AM I HERE?

*I have told you all this so that you may have peace in me. Here on earth you will have many trials and sorrows. But take heart, because I have overcome the world.*
John 16:33 NLT

*"Not again," I cried inwardly,* my body cringing.

My mother's voice sounded behind me. It began as a rough whisper, barely discernible amid the din of the store. Then it grew a bit fiercer—angrier. I turned to look at her, then quickly turned back and kept walking. I refused to look at her.

Fear and shame rose within me, overwhelming my chubby, pig-tailed self.

"Please don't get too loud, Mom," I pleaded silently to her.

I could not tell her this out loud. I dared not tell her how I felt. It had been a while since Mom spanked me. I was not about to do anything to bring on another one. Yet I dreaded the stares and snickers from the people around us.

"Just let us get back to the car soon," I mumbled, walking quicker to the door. I burst through it and kept on walking. I hated being embarrassed.

"Denise Ann! Why are you walking so fast?! Don't you see these cars out here?!"

And people turned and stared.

That was a lot of my childhood.

Whether washing dishes, watering the lawn, or walking through the store with me, my mom, Anna, would talk to herself. Sometimes she would talk to those who were invisible, uttering words that were harsh and brutal and profane and that never should be spoken within earshot of a child.

One of my mom's younger sisters lived next door to us, and I often escaped to her house to hide from my mom and the *voices*. My aunt said my mom helped raise her and their siblings after their mother left home and their dad was charged with supporting the family. A lot of the responsibility fell to my mom. My aunt thought it was too much for her. When my mom married at twenty-one and was ready to have children of her own, her body betrayed her. She miscarried several times before having me and my younger sister before she turned forty. My aunt told me that my mom had spent time in a special hospital.

This illness of the mind not only affected my mom but another sister of hers too. She acted like Mom and even worse—speaking, swearing, and shouting to people who were invisible. I remember seeing a bunch of strangers put her in a white van and drive off. People said she was going to get some medicine that would make her feel better and get better. I wondered why couldn't they do the same for my mom.

As I grew, I wondered if the same would happen to me. Would I start to hear voices? Would I speak to people who weren't there or make a spectacle of myself to the shame of those around me? How could I outrun my legacy? My mom, aunt, and, as I later learned, my paternal grandmother all suffered from mental illness. Would I suffer the same fate?

Why am I here?

I was tired. Tired of the isolation. Tired of not being able to have classmates over at my home. Tired of having my mom be mean to me. Tired of being worried about what other people thought of my family. My dad, God bless him, tried to shield me from some of the madness. He was my champion and defender. But he was hiding too. As a minister, he couldn't afford to have his ill wife and family issues exposed for his friends and colleagues and congregants to see. Like me, he kept his pain inside.

My dad was a man with two names. His mom, Fairy Mae, birthed him with the help of a midwife in rural, segregated Alabama in the late 1920s. When he was born, she turned gravely ill. She and her husband had separated months before. None of the family expected her to survive, so the family named my dad themselves . . . Robert Earl. That name stayed on his birth certificate until he amended it sixty-four years later. His mom did not die. She lived ninety-two years as a testimony to God's power to raise the dead.

When Fairy Mae regained her strength, she was livid that anyone would dare name her child. She named him LC, employing a unique southern custom of using letters in place of first names. The bonds of love between mother and son were strong, surviving sickness, separation, cross-country moves, and changing times. They were inseparable.

Like Dad and me.

We loved each other and enjoyed being together. I loved to listen to my dad reminiscence about the past. He used to tell me how his parents' separation never saddened him growing up because he felt so much love from his cousins, aunts, and uncles. He talked about life on a farm. How family members visited each other. How exciting it was to leave his small town of Georgiana and visit relatives in the big city of Birmingham. He talked about how grade school always started with Bible reading and singing in the morning. Teachers were like family. People were known. No one stayed a stranger. He talked about all the jobs he had growing up. How he helped his aunt in her store. How he worked as a newspaper boy selling the famous Black newspaper, *The Chicago Defender*. How he worked at a mill making money like a man with a family. He talked about working for a plant that made root beer and how smooth and sweet the leftover soda tasted.

My dad worked his way from janitor to jig fixer for McDonnell Douglas. He made parts to make tools used to work on the company's DC airplanes. I ran to him when he came home in the evenings. On Sundays, Dad was an evangelist and lay minister, mostly for the

Missionary Baptist Church denomination. Although he grew up surrounded by people of faith, Dad was thirty before he believed in Christ. Some workers from his job shared what it meant to be a Christian with him, and he grew to love Jesus.

Seeing my dad preach made me proud. He seemed so different, so unlike his normal self. There was a confidence and a joy to him. He flowed with the words and the music and the cries of the "amens" and "hallelujahs" of the congregants. Dad was shy. He was a short, stocky, brown-skinned man with a soft, black mustache and an unassuming demeanor—until you tickled him and made him laugh. Then he would throw back his head in humor. His eyes watered, and his whole body shook. It was a spectacle. I mean, he could get loud and embarrassing. But he made me smile.

Dad became assistant pastor at a small church in south Los Angeles. He dreamed of leading his own church. He came close. A congregation considered him and another minister to be their shepherd. They picked the other man. I sensed Dad's sadness as he told his story. I felt sorry for him.

On the weekends, Dad found solace in nature. He would load up his car—later his RV—and take Mom, my younger sister, Lanthe, and me for an outing. Sometimes Dad made the hour's drive north to Bakersfield where my mom's father, John, lived. We would talk, eat, and enjoy our visit with him in his little home. Once, we headed northeast to Littlerock, California, where there were orchards filled with fruit trees. We drove through bushland, hills, and pastures—our souls quietly soaking up the scenery. After a brief stop, we came back with lots of peaches that my mom cooked and poured into jars.

Mostly Dad took us fishing. How he loved to fish! He would prepare for his trip like he was preparing for war. He knew every rod, reel, and lure in his tackle box. He got ice for the fish he would catch and all the sodas we could drink. A special trip to the bait shop was a must. Dad would buy different types of worms or small channel cats for catching catfish. He also made sure he had enough sinkers, hooks, and bobbers because he didn't want to run out.

Then it was time to fish. Some weekends we would fish off the dock or shore at Perris Lake. The next weekend we might be in Long Beach fishing across from the Queen Mary. Another weekend we could be fishing on the beach in Rosarito, Mexico. We often fished near Indio at a place called the Salton Sea, which was not a sea but a man-made lake accidentally formed in the Coachella Valley around 1905.

I think Dad's favorite fishing place was Ross Corner in Yuma, Arizona. It was a long, slender water channel with houses set back on either side of the bushy shore. We spent Saturdays catching African perch, bass, and catfish. It was peaceful. Once in a while, you might hear a dog bark or a door creak and slam shut in the distance. And it was just ridiculously hot. At midday, nothing moved—not even the flies. I wondered why in the world Dad would drive all Friday night to fish there. Why didn't we stay in much cooler California and fish? Years later, after Mom died, I came across my parents' marriage certificate. I discovered they had wed in Yuma—a place where people went to marry before Las Vegas became popular. Yuma was close to Dad's heart. But wherever we went, I could always count on my dad to patiently fix my rod and reel, take off any fish I caught, and do it all over again.

Dad, or Papa, as I often called him, told his stories simply but powerfully. Like any good daughter, I wanted to please my dad and be like him. But I found it easier to share my thoughts and experiences on paper. Writing was my first love. I started making up stories and crafting characters for class assignments in elementary school. Even as a kindergartner, I used dialogue and quotation marks. I wanted to be Nancy Drew with a pen—solving mysteries and helping others by writing about the wrongs done to them that needed to be made right. So much lived inside me. I used writing to cut through all the barriers I felt held me back. My timidity. My dorkiness. My looks. My weight. My audible voice might be silenced through fear and people's intimidation, but no one could stop my words. My inner voice could shout unafraid.

Like my dad, I loved music. I was surrounded by music—all kinds of music. Music marked my days. On Sundays I heard Black gospel songs, spirituals, and traditional hymns. Songs like "Oh Happy Day" and "Ninety-Nine and a Half (Won't Do)," and my dad's favorite, "Blessed Assurance." Often, when Dad ran errands, he would listen to preachers on the car radio. Then I heard *White* Christian music like Sandi Patty and the Gaither Band. My mom, born and raised in Arkansas, loved country music. All day long, I heard Johnny Cash or Tammy Wynette or Merle Haggard. Thrilled I was not. But as a kid, I kept my opinions to myself. A trip to my aunt's house next door meant The Jackson Five or Barry White or BB King. Sometimes I would be brave and move my body to the beat. When I was ten, Dad gave me my own radio. That was when I discovered Elton John, Steve Miller, the Eagles, Linda Ronstadt, and all things disco—the exact opposite of what my family listened to. My relatives next door laughed and shook their heads. My dad frowned. I sheepishly lowered my head.

One day at school, something got into me. I started singing "Ben," a ballad by Michael Jackson. I liked the words about having a special friend and seeing that friend in a way that others didn't. So I opened my mouth—right there on the playground. As I sang, other kids drew near and listened. Soon a crowd encircled me. They seemed to like my singing. The next day, I sang again. More children came. I continued to sing. Sometimes people would clap when I finished. No one spoke to me, but they listened attentively. And most were friendly. Of course, some of the older boys came and kicked the back of my legs and ran off. But I kept singing. What saddened me was when my teacher spoke to me in class. "I don't want you singing every day," she ordered sternly. "It's too much for you."

Too much for me? I guess she thought I would overtire myself. Yet I felt so alive—so happy—when I sang. I never felt tired. Never. But I obeyed her warning and stopped singing. Once again, I turned inward, content to let writing and fantasizing speak to what was on my heart. The singing continued through imagining myself as the people whose songs I heard on the radio or watched on television. Over time, I became more comfortable with the characters in the world of my inner life than the real people around me. My outer scars and experiences seemed to hiss at me, telling me that I did not belong. My inner scars of self-doubt, low self-esteem, and difficulty in seeing my worth and value blinded me to who I was and why I was here. Because nothing is new under the sun, I suspect the same has happened to you.

But God causes all things to work together for good.

God showed His love for me through Papa. Despite his own sins and shortcomings, my dad reflected Christ's sacrificial care. Jesus wooed me through the stories, songs, situations, and sermons my dad shared with me. God gave me a dad who loved me and taught me the gentle, loving, protective ways of the Father. Some of you have never experienced the love of a good dad. That saddens and angers me. I am sorry for what you've been through. In this world, where child abuse, absentee parenting, and trafficking are horrible realities, it is pure grace to have had a papa like I did.

God gave me a glimpse of His purpose for me through writing and music. Only God could give words to a timid little girl and have beauty be sung from a scarred body. As a child, I thought those gifts belonged to me. I reveled in them because others saw me as worthy and valuable when I used them. But the praise of others is a snare. It traps you into thinking it is all about you. It keeps you wanting more of the praise. And if you want the praise—want the love—you try to make people want what you can give them. You must perform, and you must be perfect. You set yourself up for a mess because, ultimately, no one is going to be satisfied—not you, not the ones you hope to impress, and not God, who already loves who He made you to be. I have spent fifty-five years learning and relearning this lesson.

Dear one, learn from my experience.

Those who know Jesus have been called out of darkness and into His wonderful light to declare and show what God can do. God plans. He sets aside good things He wants us to do. It may be a smile or writing a letter to a lonely friend or singing a lullaby to a little one. The simplest offering of our time and effort can have great impact on someone's life. God can use your deed to bring hope to someone who needs it desperately. Perhaps even to you.

God has a unique purpose for each of us to accomplish. And He has promised to fulfill that purpose regardless of what we may suffer. Now let me address the obvious: I hate suffering. I loathe pain and hate seeing others in pain. I hate it when my body hurts and when I fight to sleep. I hate the disfigurement of my keloids. I hate people's rejection. It breaks my heart to be misunderstood.

God's ways and thoughts are high and often beyond me. I just know His Word says that if we share in His sufferings, we will share in His glory (Isaiah 55:11; Romans 8:17). The suffering will be our instructor, teaching us patience and endurance. God and His Word do not lie. "We must go through many hardships to enter the kingdom of God" (Acts 14:22).

God cares about our pain. He longs to bring us out of hiding and redeem our afflictions and scars. We can move forward into the future without being captive to our past. People and circumstances may help shape us, but they do not have to determine our future. What my mom, aunt, and grandmother lived through did not have to be my story. In time, I also realized I couldn't relate to God through my dad's faith or my mother's experience. I had to receive God through His Son, Jesus, for myself and walk out my own life journey.

Yes, I am my dad's daughter. And I am my mother's daughter. But more importantly, I am my Father's daughter. When I asked Jesus to be my Lord and Savior, God adopted me as His eternally beloved daughter. I am His image bearer. And He calls me good.

He calls you good too. And your existence is not in vain.

Worship has been God's special gift to me. I love to proclaim Him in song. I find that when I do, I am made more and more whole. I believe you will discover the same. Singing God's praises sets the minions fleeing and the angels of God to working. When we sing, we acknowledge the God who took our infirmities upon Himself and who promises to fulfill His purpose for us no matter what we go through.

I have had my own bouts of depression—even suicidal thoughts—but not because of my mom or aunt or anybody else—just life and my own pain and choices. We all have our own stuff. But I know

God brings healing. Whether that is through His miracles, heaven, medicine, treatment, counseling, a loving community, or, like with Elijah, rest and food, God delivers us as we partner with Him in the work of His kingdom. "He sent his word and healed them . . ." (Psalm 107:20 KJV).

### "The Lord Will Fulfill His Purpose for Me"
By Denise Ann Goosby

Life is a game full of winners and losers.
Let the games begin.
You do you, and I'll do me.
May the best one win.

It's all about me—how I feel and what I say and what I believe.
If life's a game, then let me taste sweet victory.
But what if all my playing, all my scheming
Leaves me empty, leaves me hungering after more?
What if I'm wrong?

I need something higher, something greater than myself.
I need something richer, something stronger than my fears.
I need something that my words cannot express.
God, what I need is You—fulfill Your purpose for me.

Tomorrow is a promise that may never come.
If I'm living for today, well, what's the hope in that, oh ah.
Life's too fast and furious to leave it in my hands.
Time has got to count—I've got to live, oh, I've got to take a stand.

Give me meaning for my hurt and my pain.
Bring me healing—deliver me again.
Let my love ring out like a battle hymn.
Don't let this life I'm living be spent in selfish gain.

I need something higher, something greater than myself.
I need something richer, something stronger than my fears,
I need something that my words cannot express,
God, what I need is You, fulfill Your purpose for me.

I need something higher, something greater than myself.
I need something higher, something stronger than my fears.
I need something that my words cannot express.
God, what I need is You—fulfill Your purpose for me.

Fulfill Your purpose in me . . .
Fulfill Your purpose in me . . .
Fulfill Your purpose in me . . .

© Denise Ann Goosby 2020

### Devotion

### My Father's Child

*Thus we have been set free to experience our rightful heritage. You can
tell for sure that you are now fully adopted as his own children because
God sent the Spirit of his Son into our lives crying out, "Papa! Father!"*
Galatians 4:5–6 MSG

Hallelujah! The old has gone and the new has come (2 Corinthians
5:17). We are better than new. God's Spirit dwells within us. We live
and move and have our being in Him (Acts 17:28). And whether we
do or do not struggle with mental illness, we have the mind of Christ
(1 Corinthians 2:14). Our inner and outer scars do not define us or
plot our course. Nothing—not our infirmities, our issues, or our weaknesses—can separate us from God and His love.

God is Jehovah Rapha, the God who heals. He called us to Himself
even when we were sinners. Even when we feared Him. Even when we
rejected Him. He did that for me. He will for you too. God does not
call us to be super Christians. You and I are flawed, prone to wander
and rebel. Yet God's Spirit will help us be faithful. Remember, we are in
process. We walk out our salvation in reverence to God. We need to stay
in God's Word and ask Him to help us hear His voice and do His will.

> I'd say you'll do best by filling your minds and meditating
> on things true, noble, reputable, authentic, compelling,
> gracious—the best, not the worst; the beautiful, not the ugly;
> things to praise, not things to curse. (Philippians 4:8 MSG)

You are not your wounds and scars. You are not your addic-
tions and struggles. You are not your status or condition. You are

God's beloved, created to do wonderful things that He prepared and anointed you to do. Your competence is in Him.

You are good enough.

Do those things that draw you closer to Him. Serve God by serving others in His name. Immerse yourself in nature, art, and music. Look for and acknowledge the beauty around you—especially that which lies within yourself.

### Questions to Ponder in Your Heart

What are some experiences from your family history that have shaped you? What does God's Word say about who you should pattern yourself after? What can bring peace and transformation, especially in your mind?

### Prayer

*Father, You made me and call me good.* I am Yours. Even in my weakness, infirmity, and sin, You call me beloved. Lord, fulfill Your purpose for me. Let me use my gifts, talents, abilities, and treasure for Your glory. Please comfort me. Manifest Your peace in me. Bring me healing and strength for my days. Remind me that You love me just as I am. I give myself to You. Make me more and more like Jesus. And use me for Your glory. Bless me indeed, Father. In Jesus's name I pray, Amen.

### Memory Verse

> The LORD will fulfill his purpose for me; your steadfast love,
> O LORD, endures forever. Do not forsake the work of your
> hands. (Psalm 138:8 ESV)

# Chapter 3

# WHAT WILL HAPPEN TO ME?

*I can't help but wonder why You care about mortals—sons and daughters of men—specks of dust floating about the cosmos.*
Psalm 8:4 VOICE

*I had always thought of* my aunt's house next door as a refuge—a place where I could hide from the neighborhood bullies and Mom's voices. One night I sat watching as my aunt, uncle, and cousins played cards at the dining room table. Card playing never appealed to me, but it was something to do, and I could watch everyone talk and laugh and slap cards down on the table.

I remember standing in front of the window facing the table. I looked up to see my oldest cousin staring at me. He started laughing. His eyes were glassy. I think he had been drinking. That's when I saw the gun in his hand. For a few moments, there was a standoff—his eyes on me and my eyes on the gun. No one spoke. It was still. Someone laughed nervously. I think my aunt might have called his name.

He smiled, but the gun somehow was no longer in his hand. He had gotten my attention. He had scared me. More nervous laughter followed as people settled into their seats. The card game resumed, and I continued to watch them. I did not know to do anything different. People glanced at me, but no one spoke. Eventually I went home.

What happened stayed in that room. I never mentioned that night to anyone—certainly not to those who were there. I just went on with my life. Yes, I returned to visit them many times. I protected myself and kept silent. *Would it matter if I said something? What would happen to me?*

That question came up again months later. A pain grew in my left hip. For several weeks, I tried to walk and play and go to school. But I developed a serious limp. My parents took me to a hospital nearby. Doctors examined me and ran tests. One of them spoke to my dad in the hallway outside my examination room. Dad seemed to be pleading with him. He was afraid. I was afraid.

When it was time to leave, a nurse told my dad not to let me run. Distracted, my dad walked out of the hospital with me trailing behind. He reached his RV and settled in beside my mom, apparently explaining to her what the doctor had said. I wanted to know what was wrong with me. I started to move my legs, trying to run. "No. Don't run!" my parents admonished, trying not to sound alarmed.

Later I learned that I would need an operation. Blood clots had formed in my left leg. Pins needed to be placed in my hip, and soon— if not, I could lose my leg. I learned something else too. My mom had discovered a lump in her breast shortly before my own diagnosis. I never heard the word *cancer* mentioned. A few days later, my mom and I both checked into the hospital for surgery—me for the clots and her for a mastectomy. I remember seeing my mom being pushed away in a wheelchair. Then I was taken to my own room. It would be nearly a month before I saw her again.

My dad, sister, and aunts came to visit me. From my aunts and sister, I learned that my dad had a hard time dealing with his wife and daughter being in the hospital. He worried for my mom and me. He worried if his insurance would pay all the medical bills. My sister said that when he came to pick her up at school, she saw tears streaming down his face.

My time in the hospital was a whirlwind of doctor visits and tests . . . and shame. Puberty came quickly for me. At ten, I started my period and had a woman's curves. And I was heavy. I didn't mind so much when the lady nurses were with me. Sometimes they kept me company by watching television or chatting with each other for a few minutes in my room. A few peeked into my room as they walked the halls during their shifts. My heart fell when any men came in. I felt exposed and wanting. I missed home.

My stay in the hospital lasted about a week. My left hip now throbbed with a different kind of pain that eventually faded. I looked forward to going home. My dad's mom had come to help him take care of my sister and the household. It would be nice to see her too. Yet taking care of me and my sister while working was too much for my dad. Instead of bringing me home, Dad had me stay with an aunt and uncle on the other side of town. They took care of me until my mom came home a week later. Thankfully, Mom and I recovered from our surgeries—though my mom always carried a sadness about her beyond what she bore with mental illness. Dad's insurance miraculously paid for all our care. God graciously provided and spared our family from further trauma and financial hardship.

Yet the experience altered me.

A long, thin scar on my left hip now joined the small scars that continued to manifest on my upper body. It took me a long time to heal and walk normally. Even then, my left leg became slightly shorter than my right leg, so I wobbled. My surgery and rehab meant I had to be homeschooled by the school district. A teacher came several times a week to give lessons and to check my work. I loved it. I could do my studies, write stories, and be safe from the mean kids at school.

It also made it easier for me to hide and isolate myself from others. I no longer wanted to be with kids my age. It was hard being around my mom and the voices, but if it meant no bullying, I would be okay. Even after I healed and returned to the neighborhood school to graduate from sixth grade, I was determined to protect myself from what I imagined junior high would be for a heavy, shy kid with a limp. I convinced my doctor that walking to school and participating in activities would tax me. "You need to socialize," he told me, slowing his words as he looked at me. He pursed his lips and signed the papers for me to resume homeschooling.

To me, him signing the papers was an act of grace and survival. I suspect it was not God's perfect will for me to stay home, but I do know He used the homeschooling for good. He used it to increase my love for writing and learning, stirring up gifts He had already given me. He also used homeschooling to introduce new people into my life who challenged and encouraged me.

I am forever grateful that God brought a spunky red-haired Jewish teacher named Tobi Hornbein into my life. I always smiled when Mrs. Hornbein walked through my door. I usually got nervous when people came over. Dysfunction ruled my house. My mom's mental illness and health struggles made it difficult for her to connect with anyone except family. Her mental health also kept her from keeping the house clean and orderly. Dad worked and my sister went to school. Although I was home, doing domestic chores never interested me. Mom also hoarded things (a practice I later acquired), so our two-bedroom abode overflowed with stuff. That meant I ended up sleeping on the living room couch.

Into this household Mrs. Hornbein bravely stepped and kept coming. She just asked that a place be made available for us to have class. Sometimes it was at the kitchen or dining room table, but mostly we held class on the couch in the living room, which also served as my bed at night. She and I talked history, did math problems, and discussed stories I wrote. She loved my stories and thought I was a good writer. She also thought I was spoiled. She knew I feared people, and she implored me to get out of my house and do things. I wanted that for myself too.

I sensed Mrs. Hornbein saw inside me. She got a glimpse of my heart and cared enough to enter my world of dysfunction. She was a storyteller too. My eyes never left her face as she described her time in the civil rights movement marching with Dr. King. She wanted me to grow up and do well in school so I could write her life's story. I feel sad when I think about her now. She gave me so much, and I gave her so little. Writing her story would have been the least I could do.

Time picked up speed as I neared high school. Homeschooling ended. No more doctor's notes would be written. I could no longer hide. I prepared to enter a nearby public high school. I would deal with whatever I had to deal with. But I still dreaded the change to come. My aunt next door feared for me. "Why does she have to go there?" she cried anxiously, concerned about how my schoolmates might treat me.

One day, she and her daughter took me to Regina Caeli. Caeli was a tiny all-girl Catholic high school a few miles from my house. It sat across the street from St. Albert the Great school and church. I remember looking at the pictures of the nuns hanging on the walls of the main office. I noticed all the nuns were Black. I had never seen a Black nun before. Later I learned that they came from an all-Black religious order in Louisiana called Sisters of the Holy Family. The sister who spoke with my aunt and me seemed businesslike but kind. She sent us away with papers for my dad to sign and instructions for buying books and a uniform. I sat quietly, wondering how this would work out. Could Dad even afford to send me here?

Papa never said I could go. But days later, he handed me checks to pay for my books and the first month of classes. I entered Regina Caeli as a sophomore and stayed there until I graduated three years later as valedictorian. God says in the Bible that He seeks out and prepares places for us—unexpected places. Caeli was an oasis for me that nurtured my love for learning and writing.

God sends people into our lives. He sent me Mavis Myers who taught me French and Latin at Caeli. I respected her immensely. A short, sturdy German American woman with stoic Amish-like faith, Mavis was stern and loving. She respectfully spoke her mind. She could laugh with you and set you straight. Mavis and I shared a love of writing, the *Star Wars* trilogy, and Dodgers baseball.

I remember she asked me to spend the weekend with her and her dad at their house in Downey. It was eight miles away in distance and much further from my home in culture. Both had a tinge of suburbia and a strong working-class bent, but Downey was mostly Anglo, conservative, and still holding on to vestiges of its dairy and agricultural past. The houses seemed bigger with a lot of land surrounding them.

When Mavis drove me to her place, her dad was on a small tractor in their backyard finishing up his work for the day. We said hello, walked up the front porch, and went inside. I was excited, though I did not say so to Mavis. I had never had someone invite me to their house for a visit before. Mavis took me to a spare bedroom. I looked at the quilts and dolls and old-fashioned furniture and knickknacks that filled it. I could not believe this pretty place would be mine for the weekend.

My favorite part of the stay was when Mavis, her dad, and I would sit down at their table and eat. We did not do this at my house. I enjoyed the peace and simple joy of talking with others and sharing their company. To this day, it is one of my favorite things to do.

After dinner the first night, Mavis went to visit a neighbor across the street. She started to invite me, then hesitated. "Maybe . . . maybe you should stay here," she decided. That was fine with me. I liked being in her house. A few minutes later, Mavis startled me.

"You stay here for now. I need to talk to Dad," she commanded firmly. She was a bit breathless with a determined set to her chin. I could hear her and her dad's muffled voices. I could not make out much of what they said. But I did know they were not happy.

I found out why the next morning when Mavis called me into her living room and invited me to sit down across from her. She explained that her neighbor did not like that Mavis had me in her house. "She said you would bring down the property value of the houses in the neighborhood." So that was why Mavis decided not to take me over there last night. Her neighbor could not handle Mavis bringing one of her black students to visit. And Mavis was livid, choosing to vent to her dad before speaking to me.

The whole situation disappointed me. It irked Mavis greatly. But she still invited me over a couple of times. When she moved out of state, we still talked over the phone about things like our families, church life, and teaching.

Mavis planned to return to Southern California to start an urban teaching ministry. I looked forward to seeing her. But one Sunday evening, her sister called me and said Mavis had died of a heart attack—at fifty. How quickly life can end. How impactful one life can be! Both truths should encourage us to see how precious our lives and legacies can be to those around us.

Caeli's teachers and students taught me how to speak to people and relate to them. I still feared people, but anxiety about the future motivated me to achieve. I knew I needed an education. I needed to go to college and get a job that would sustain my life.

The keloids on my chest and back became more prominent. According to Harvard University Health, keloids appear in people ages ten to thirty. For women, puberty and pregnancy increase the likelihood that keloids would form and progress.[4] I realized my condition probably would not improve. To me, my keloids and weight meant no man would want me as a wife. No one would want to care for someone scarred and lacking beauty.

But the desire for romance and companionship grew. I decided to act. I wanted my keloids removed. I talked with a doctor who examined me and agreed to do the surgery. It would mean enduring the pain of an operation and weeks of steroid shots. I hesitated but decided that freedom from keloids would be worth what I might endure. My dad had the same hope. He thought surgery would help me by keeping me from being self-conscious.

I had just started college. Like every young woman, I wanted to fit in. I wanted to make new friends, have a boyfriend, and be like everyone else. No matter what age we are, we never want to be *that*

4  Harvard Health Publishing Harvard Medical School "Keloids" April 2019 healthharvard.edu

*one*—the one who is different, the one who seems misplaced. As a plus-sized African American girl at a mostly white college in Southern California, I wanted one thing . . . to be accepted.

But what Papa and I failed to grasp at the time was that surgery to remove keloids in the late '80s was not the best thing. Keloids often grow back. Surgery only introduced more trauma to my body—trauma that resulted in more scarring and more keloids. An infection had also set in. I still remember the look of concern and disappointment on the doctor's face as he treated it. Not even the shots were enough to stop the scarring. I had counted the cost and had come out the worse for it.

I wondered, *What would happen to me now?*

"Oh, I will sing of the goodness of God."

I linger in the shower, not ready to stop singing—not wanting to face the familiar routine of cleaning and bandaging my wound. The pressure that built up in my chest and back the past few days is gone now. *Thank You, God. Maybe tonight I can get a little more sleep.* My spirit lifts with the thought. These days, I try to be quicker to count the blessings and the good things that come my way. I know what God has already brought me through. Yet even in the face of God's faithfulness, I still ask, "What will happen to me?"

You ask it too, don't you?

The desire to know the future does not diminish with time or age. Sometimes I think I disappoint God—that my distrust angers Him. I imagine Him shaking His head at me. I fear He will punish me for my lack of faith by sending more trials my way—trials I cannot handle. But that is not the heart of God. That is not what God's Word tells me about how God feels about me or about you. I am starting to see that God may be most disappointed when I misjudge Him.

In my fear, I see God as someone who wants to harm me. In my doubts, I see God as someone who will withhold love from me. In my trials, I see Him as someone who will abandon me. But God will do none of those things:

Praise the LORD, my soul; all my inmost being, praise his holy name. Praise the LORD, my soul, and forget not all his benefits—who forgives all your sins and heals all your diseases, who redeems your life from the pit and crowns you with love and compassion, who satisfies your desires with good things so that your youth is renewed like the eagle's. (Psalm 103:1–5)

The Lord knows what will happen to you and me. And He shoots straight. God tells us that we will know struggle and hardship and pain. The effects of Adam's curse on us—God's beloved creation—remains. Sin scarred us before we entered this world. On our best day, we fall short. In all our striving and grasping for control, we will still have to go through what we go through. That is not what I want to hear, but this truth resonates in my spirit.

Thankfully, this is where God lavishes us with His grace. He starts by giving us Himself. God promises to be with us. He assures us that nothing can snatch us out of His hand (John 10:29). God knows all our days. And those days will be followed by His goodness and mercy (Psalm 139:16; Psalm 23:6). God will speak to us. Whether we turn to the right or left, He will tell us the way to go. God will not reject us. He is faithful when we are not and lovingly meets with us in our fears.

Have I not commanded you? Be strong and courageous. Do not be frightened, and do not be dismayed, for the LORD your God is with you wherever you go. (Joshua 1:9 ESV)

Because our ultimate destination is Him, God will get us where we need to go. He promises to help us through the twists and turns of our journey. God knew this life was too much for us to bear on our own. Again, He gave us Himself. His Holy Spirit lives in those who believe in His Son, Jesus. His Spirit teaches, counsels, and guides us. Through the Spirit we have the mind and wisdom of Christ. All we have to do is ask, and God supplies all we need for body, soul, and spirit. God defends and protects us. He fights our battles, defeats our enemies, and causes us to triumph. Our God is a warrior (Exodus 15:3). His desire is for us.

> "Though the mountains be shaken and the hills be removed, yet my unfailing love for you will not be shaken nor my covenant of peace be removed," says the LORD, who has compassion on you. (Isaiah 54:10)

This compassionate God knows every detail of our lives. He knows who will hurt us. He knows who we will hurt. He knows the harm the choices of others—or our own—will do to us. He knows the afflictions that will come our way. He knows. Good or bad, God will use the things that happen to us for good. God will work out His plans for my life. He will complete what He has begun in me. But I must walk out those plans and purposes. I have more to do. More to learn. More to experience.

"Your goodness is running after . . . it's running after me . . ."

I sing the bridge of the song with a little more energy now. Time to see what the rest of the day holds. Soon I will gather my journal and Bible and sit quietly before God and listen to what He speaks to me. I need Him. I need Him to refresh me, to strengthen me. I need Him to reassure me that baring my scars is not in vain. I need the beauty of His Word and the beauty of His presence to see the beauty in this life I am living.

The journey continues.

### "The Promise"

By Denise Ann Goosby

Be still, the promise is near,
O my soul.
Be still, the promise is near,
O my soul.

Don't give up now . . .
It soon will come.
Don't you fear . . .
What matters now . . .

(Is to) keep on believing and trust in the Lord right now.
Keep on believing and know He's working it out.
God cannot fail, and He does not lie.
He'll do what He promised in His own time.
You'll see His glory and praise His name.
Just believe.

**Devotion**

**God Gives Me Himself**

*I am the light of the world. Whoever follows me will not walk in darkness, but will have the light of life.*
John 8:12 ESV

God is what we need the most as we live our scar-filled yet beautiful lives.

Look at Joshua. After Moses died, Joshua had to face life without the man he had served for forty years, the man whom God used to deliver the Jewish people from slavery with signs and miracles. Now God had charged Joshua—an old man in his eighties—with leading the Hebrew people into battle for the promised land. Joshua would be the *new Moses*. He was terrified.

Yet through God's dealings with Joshua, He shows us how He empowers us to navigate the happenings in our lives. Change was coming. Joshua and the Jewish people had to prepare. God promised He would be with them and would act on their behalf.

God is concerned about you too. God is also with you. No matter your pains, your mess, or your scars, God promises to walk with you every moment and every day of your life.

> As I was with Moses, so I will be with you; I will never leave
> you nor forsake you. (Joshua 1:5b)

Even with God at our side, life can be scary—especially when our experiences leave scars. Three times in Joshua 1, verses 6, 7, and 9, God implored Joshua to "be strong and courageous." He told Joshua to press on even though he felt afraid. God wanted Joshua freed from emotion. Likewise, God doesn't want us to be held captive by what scares us. He doesn't want our scars to be our chains.

Joshua had been beside Moses for decades. Even with his own life and experiences, there was still so much that Joshua needed to know. God directed him—and He implores you and me today—to read, study, think about, and do what is written in His Word.

> Keep this Book of the Law always on your lips; meditate on it day and night, so that you may be careful to do everything written in it. Then you will be prosperous and successful. (Joshua 1:8)

Stay in God's Word and look to Him for guidance. There is no other way.

**Questions to Ponder in Your Heart**
How has God shown that He is with you?
What Bible verse means the most to you?
What would you do if you were not afraid?

**Prayer**
*Father God, You and You alone know what will happen to me.* My future is in Your loving hands. Father, sometimes I get tired. My pain and circumstances seem insurmountable. But You are my God. You are a big God. You love me. You care for me. You will provide all that I need, including strength for my days. I belong to You, and You will not abandon me. Thank You for being my all and all. Amen.

**Memory Verse**

> When you pass through the waters, I will be with you; and when you pass through the rivers, they will not sweep over you. When you walk through the fire, you will not be burned; the flames will not set you ablaze. (Isaiah 43:2)

# Chapter 4

# HOW DO I MAKE A LIFE?

*Leave your country, your family, and your father's home for a land
that I will show you.*
Genesis 12:1 MSG

*I'm finally escaping the chaos,* I thought as I surveyed the living room. Glancing upward, I smiled. It seemed impossible this day would come when I was a little girl, trapped and surrounded by so much stuff, all of Mom's voices, and my own fear. During college, I lived on campus during the week, a brief respite before returning home Friday nights to face family challenges both familiar and new.

Illness had struck our family like a whirlwind once again. Dad's blood pressure was hard to control. It left him bedridden for several days before he felt well enough to go back to work. Sometimes he would get nosebleeds when it flared up again. It made it easier for him to accept retirement when it came at sixty-four. Unfortunately, Dad spent much of the early part of his retirement caring for his mother. Old age and hard years finally caught up to her. She spent her time in bed at a local convalescent home. All she wanted was her son. Dad visited her nearly every day. She would not eat unless he brought her food. When she passed, a piece of his soul went with her. You could see it in his eyes—how he carried himself. Somehow he had been lessened.

Then my mom's health started to decline. Her feet and legs became swollen and painful. One night she suffered an attack and almost passed out. Paramedics came and rushed her to the hospital. Days of tests revealed heart trouble that doctors said only a new valve could cure. She chose not to have it. Her last surgery left her without a breast. Perhaps she didn't want to deal with another loss.

A few years before, my younger sister, Lanthe, was diagnosed with lupus—a life-threatening autoimmune disease where the body attacks itself, damaging internal organs and causing fatigue and pain. "My life is just ruined," Lanthe said to me as we ran errands one day. She couldn't understand why God allowed sickness into her life. I sat quietly. What could I say? I had my own questions and fears about God. Honestly, I felt guilty about what she was going through.

My sister and I were more adversaries than friends. We lived our own lives and tried to stay out of the other's way. Lanthe thought my parents favored me over her. She said as much. I thought the same. I was the good girl who got good grades and obeyed her parents. She was the rebellious younger sibling who sometimes flouted the rules. Now she was sick, in and out of the hospital and unable to work. Soon her kidneys would shut down, and she would be on dialysis for several years. Deep down I feared I would get lupus too.

Despite the sickness and uncertainty that hovered over my family, I moved on. It was time for me to live on my own. After graduating from college and grad school, I worked a few years as a reporter for a local newspaper called the *News Tribune*. I dreamed of working my way up to being city editor of the *Los Angeles Times*. A decrease in advertising money triggered layoffs at the paper.

*How do I take care of myself without a job?* I wondered. *How do I make a life?*

The God I feared as a girl and ignored as a young woman worked through my circumstances. Covering school board meetings and interviewing people for the newspaper stirred an interest in education. I took and passed the CBEST, which candidates needed in California before they could teach. I began teaching high school diploma and English as

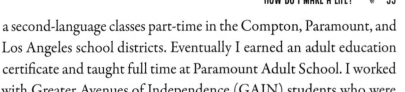

a second-language classes part-time in the Compton, Paramount, and Los Angeles school districts. Eventually I earned an adult education certificate and taught full time at Paramount Adult School. I worked with Greater Avenues of Independence (GAIN) students who were on government assistance and working toward a diploma or general education diploma (GED). It thrilled me to watch my students, mostly young women and mothers, learning and working hard. I loved seeing them be successful. It encouraged me to know I could help them and play a part in their success.

When a drop in student enrollment left me with fewer hours and a cut in pay, I felt confident as I applied to be an elementary substitute for the Los Angeles school district. The lady who interviewed me forever changed the direction of my life. On a whim, I had taken a national teacher's test a few months before. I was still waiting for my results. "If you pass, you can join our teacher internship program," she told me earnestly. Interns taught under supervision while taking district classes and performing projects and other activities. Completion of the program resulted in a California teaching credential.

I started teaching kindergarten at Nevin Avenue Elementary School five months after the interview. Two years later, I was credentialed. Three years later, I bought a house through a program sponsored by the city of Compton and the Nehemiah Housing Corporation. My dad and I had planned to buy the house together, but the realtor said I could buy it on my own. I expected my family to move in with me. But months passed. Silently, Dad changed his mind. Looking back, I could see he did not want to give up his house no matter how chaotic and cluttered it was. He worked hard for it. It cost him. He and Mom were one of the first Black families in their Compton neighborhood in the late fifties. He bought the house using the GI Bill. To him, it was more than just a home.

To me, it was something different.

Yes, it was a home. It was a place where my dad's love nourished and sustained me. Through him, I heard God's Word and saw Dad live out his faith. It was a place where Mrs. Hornbein encouraged my learning and writing. And it was a safe harbor that protected me from the neighborhood bullies.

Yet it was my prison too. It was a place of secrets. A place where doors slammed. A place where anger could elicit cutting words or a well-placed hand or object on flesh. And, of course, Mom's voices competed with country music as the soundtrack to my childhood. It was a place of fear. Fear of people. Fear of the world outside its walls. Fear of the unknown.

How do you make a life in such a place?

By the grace of God, I had made a life there for thirty-three years. But no more. I anxiously gathered up the last of my belongings and paused. I was leaving a home and a life I had always known. I understood why Dad wanted to stay. Slowly I opened the front screen door and stepped onto the porch. I saw my mom's wind chimes hanging above the rail and smiled. I loved those wind chimes. I loved the music they made when the wind blew through as the afternoon sea breeze kicked up. A gentle tinkle would sound, and as the wind rose, all the little chimes would sing together.

*Maybe I will put some up at my new place.* They brought peace to my mom. Like Saul being comforted by David's harp, the wind chimes soothed my mom's spirit. Funny. I never did end up getting wind chimes. They would not have meant the same for me anyway. They sang my mother's song—a song of a soul held captive by an inner world filled with pain and anguish. Another melody sang in my spirit. I could put no words to it yet. But somehow its tune moved me forward away from the familiar and into the unknown. I had no choice but to see where it led.

"Are you okay? What's the matter?" Frowning, Gloria walked over and stood in front of me. I tried to speak, but all I could do was look at her. It felt like part of my chest was being ripped open.

"I'm not feeling very well," I answered, struggling to keep myself upright in the chair.

I looked around at the little bodies working diligently on the computers in front of them. Gloria and I co-taught a morning and afternoon kindergarten class. Today was our weekly trip to the computer lab. It was typically a time for us to catch our breath and enjoy our young pupils before continuing with the day, but now I wondered if I could make it through the class.

"Why don't you go home?" Gloria admonished me.

Good question.

The pain in my chest had been building for several days. The skin around some of the keloids on my chest turned red and felt hot to the touch. Since the surgery, some had slowly moved and joined together, forming scar tissue that itched. Creams and lotions soothed for a moment, but the itching remained. Now pressure in my chest was building. I was scared. Scared for what was happening to me physically. Scared for how I might be perceived and handled by the people who would treat me. Scared I would be wounded by another caregiver.

A few years ago, I visited a new primary doctor. For whatever reason, I had to disrobe and expose my keloids. She tried to be professional, but the sight of my scars shocked her. Then she became a scientist. She asked questions. Took measurements. And snapped pictures. I think she wanted some of her colleagues to examine me and asked me if it was okay.

I looked at her and mumbled. Words stuck in my throat. I felt so much, but shame and fear silenced my voice. To me, it would have been unseemly to speak out. Maybe I felt I would have lost it and started raging. I just wanted out. After a few more minutes, I got dressed and left the office.

Once home, I sat down and wrote a letter about how embarrassed and hurt I felt and sent it to her. It took me a long time to get up the courage to face her again. To the doctor's credit, she greeted me with a hug and a kiss and apologized for how she made me feel. I was thankful for her kind words and gentle touch. Yet the encounter left a mark. It played into the voices within and around me that said I was damaged and ugly.

I did not want to risk going to see a doctor, but I had to. The pain and pressure continued even after I left the computer lab, finished school, and made the drive home. The feeling persisted a few days later, and I noticed a break in my skin and blood and puss coming out. Horrified, I scheduled an appointment with a dermatologist. She diagnosed an infection. I winced as she cleaned and dressed the wound. "Why don't you let me shoot them and try to get them down?" she asked, looking at my scars.

A common treatment for keloids is to inject them with steroids. The idea is to shrink them to make them less noticeable and impactful for the patient. Steroids mean weekly shots into each keloid for months. And because the scarring can be hard and unyielding, the needle has to go deep within the keloid. My scarring covered a significant part of my body including my face, thanks to a bout with adult chicken pox when I was in grad school.

"We should try to get them down," she repeated.

I shook my head. The shots seemed like torture to me. I had some after my surgery to remove some of my keloids, but they still came back.

"No. No. I don't want to," I finally responded.

It felt like I was giving up, forever rejecting a chance to be made whole and beautiful and live a normal life. It was out of the question. So I moved on, pouring myself into teaching and thankful that I could support myself. Making a life depended on me, on what I could do, and what I could get. I would never have beauty, but I could have success. Afterall, I already lived the *American dream*. I owned a home. I had a career. My family and colleagues respected me. It would have to be enough.

It took a colleague to remind me that there was more to life than being successful. A tall, elegantly dressed woman with a hint of southern in her voice encouraged me in everything I did. Often we laughed about things we encountered at work, or we talked about things we saw in the news. One day, I slipped into her office to chat. She asked me a question.

"Do you go to church?" she asked, looking at me earnestly.

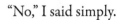

"No," I said simply.

"Do you think maybe you owe God one hour a week of your time?"

Silently, I considered what she said. God had not crossed my thoughts for a long time. Not that way. I knew He loved my dad. I mean, my dad was a minister and assistant pastor. Our extended family turned to Dad when people were sick or a funeral had to be conducted. Dad handled the God stuff.

But if God was God—almighty and all powerful—I had to agree with her. He was certainly worth an hour a week of my time. The next Sunday, I pulled up outside an ornate white church in south Los Angeles. Compared to the tiny storefront or house churches I attended with my dad as a child, this church seemed huge. It easily seated a couple hundred people. A small sea of suited and brightly dressed parishioners greeted me as I walked in. I searched for my friend but didn't see her. I looked around and noticed the murals on the walls and the choir members on the stage. I didn't hear the "amens" and "hallelujahs" I often heard in my dad's church. No dancing or hopping up and down. These people were quiet but attentive. They reminded me of the people who attended the Catholic church across the street from my high school. Dad would leave me there on his way to work in the morning. Except for a funeral, it was the last church I visited. Until now.

I saw her as I was leaving. She asked how I liked her church. I told her I would be back, but, secretly, I had no desire to return. I had fulfilled an obligation and done my duty of something I thought I had to do. But her question about giving God an hour seemed reasonable to me. That question, coupled with seeing my dad pray, sing, and read his Bible, did something in me. I thought about the future. I thought about life without my family. I thought about being alone. Dad and Mom were getting older. My sister needed dialysis three times a week. Mom could barely walk and rarely left home. Dad had retired but dealt with high blood pressure. I was coming to grips with the fact that my family would not be around much longer.

*How would I make a life without them?*

At this point, I knew I needed help. I decided to find a New Life Clinic and see a Christian counselor. I learned about the clinics when I watched the Trinity Broadcasting Network with my dad. I had seen a counselor briefly while I was in college. But now I wanted God involved. I wanted Him to direct the person guiding me. The kind, elderly counselor God placed in my life gave me hope. She listened to me and encouraged me. She let me speak and give voice to what I had done and some of the things done to me. With her I could share about things that frightened me. Tentatively, through her, I continued to seek God despite my fear of Him. I shared with her that I wanted to find a large multicultural church where I could meet people and participate in different activities. While we talked, I pictured myself driving by a church at Figueroa and Torrance. I had passed by it several times. Not once did I think about stopping . . . until then.

One Sunday I parked my black hatchback on the dirty backdrop that served as the church's parking lot. I sat for a moment. Other cars parked around me. People opened doors and greeted each other. I heard laughter and shoes crunching on the pavement. I sensed the friendliness in the atmosphere. Yet I felt disconcerted and out of place. No one looked like me—no brown or black skin.

I opened the door and stepped out into the fall morning air and walked the short distance to the brown building ahead of me. It looked like an office building. In fact, the whole area was a series of little buildings that contained businesses, and, as I later learned, contained several other churches, including an African American one. As I walked through the door, someone handed me a booklet and directed me inside.

I sat and took in the scene of bodies standing, sitting, hugging, and laughing. On the front wall I saw the black outline of a dove. *Hmm. Interesting. So different from what I had experienced in the past.* People stood as music started to play. It captivated me. It was not the gospel songs of my childhood or the Catholic hymns from high school. It was closer to the pop-rock songs I listened to on FM radio, only these songs talked about God and loving Him. I cannot recall the preacher or his message. But those songs spoke powerfully to me.

The music drew me.

I continued to go to the church off and on for several months. I noticed there were a few African Americans and other people of color. I also saw that the church had a bookstore. The bulletin listed several activities and programs. It started to resemble the place I had longed for in my counselor's office. The day came when I realized why I had been led there. Yes, the beauty of the songs wooed me. Yes, I grew more comfortable with the people. And perhaps it was nice to have a second family to look to when my biological one felt so fragile.

But I believed.

I believed in God, I believed in His Son, Jesus. I believed that He died to pay for the wrong things I did. I believed He died for me, and if I asked Him to lead, guide, and empower me through His Spirit, He would help me live my life. So when the minister asked who wanted Jesus, I stood up, walked forward, and joined hands with him and several others and said a prayer. A few minutes later, a gentleman ushered me and several others to another room nearby where lay counselors prayed for and spoke with us. A blonde-haired woman named Christine spoke to me. I recognized her as one of the church's missionaries. She encouraged me to attend new life class where I would learn what Christianity was about and how to live as a Christian. I hesitated. "How would going to class affect my family?"

"You'll be better able to help your family," she responded simply.

I took the paper she offered about the class and looked to see when it was scheduled. It was another opportunity to step into the unknown. I am glad I moved forward. For the next twelve weeks, I met with a group of other new Christians and learned about reading the Bible, talking to God, serving other people, and growing in my faith. It was the best thing I could have done. I learned how important it was to spend time on my own reading the Bible and talking to God. I had to get to know Him. I had to learn who He was, what He was like, how He thought about me, and what He expected of me. My dad, colleagues, counselors, and my pastor could only take me so far. I had to walk with and experience God for myself.

It was a new beginning. It was a new way of relating to the world and to others. God had to be in charge now. My life had to be lived by what He taught me from the Bible and His Spirit, who now lived inside me. Happiness and success depended on developing a heart in tune with God—a heart that pursued Him and what He cared about. Life was not about my job, my money, my reputation, or my looks. Nor was it about my past. Life began and ended with God—with the changes and work He would do in and through me.

*God can do anything,* I repeated.

With God, I can make a life. The concept still seemed daunting. What would God do? How would He do it? I knew more hard stuff was coming. But I had hope now. I looked forward to what God might do. I looked forward to new experiences and new people. Would He heal my keloids? The possibility thrilled me. God does miracles. He heals people. Why not me? Perhaps I no longer needed to be afraid of being alone. Perhaps I could have close friends who loved me and wanted to do fun things with me. Maybe some man would want to marry me. Besides, I belong to God. He can give favor and open doors.

I had to look to Him.

The inner and outer scars I carried did not have to define me. They do not have to define you. Life is made when we learn—through time, trial, error, and triumph—to listen to, trust in, and obey God. Life changes when we believe that He really does love us and wants the best for us. In his eighties, Dad told me that Matthew 6:33 was a Scripture all Christians needed to live: "Seek first the kingdom of God and His righteousness, and all these other things will be added unto you." Dad regretted the times when his life did not reflect that verse. "It's the best bargain anyone can have," he said.

Dad reminded me that Christians often forget where our help comes from. We forget that every good thing we have comes from God alone. And that even the best things on earth will not make us happy. Galatians 2:20 says we "have been crucified with Christ." Our old life before we knew Jesus does not exist anymore. In the old life, we called the shots. We believed what we wanted to believe, did what we wanted to do, and lived for self.

In many ways, life is a struggle between what we desire and what God desires for us. Frankly, what God wants for me I may not want. I fight against the things He allows to happen. God's ways are often beyond me. I wish I had never developed keloids. I wish my mom didn't hear voices or my sister contract lupus. I wish my dad could have had his own church and that his mom would have lived longer. But God is in control. I am not my own. I belong to Him. If you follow Christ, you belong to Him too. We must let God live life through us. He must move and have His being within us so we become more like Him.

God creates and gives life. He knows how to live it. He says life is not what we have or what title we carry. Life is living by His words written in the Bible. Life is being led by His Spirit instead of our feelings and circumstances. Life is making the most of our time on earth, knowing God, and making Him known in these perilous days. Life is giving self away in loving God and others the way Jesus did. God makes life worth living. Without Him, we have no life:

> Whoever has the Son has life; whoever does not have the
> Son does not have life. (1 John 5:12)

Psalm 127:1 says that unless God is in the making, those who work labor in vain. Such are the lives we live. Without God, there is no beauty. Without God, there is no purpose. Without God, there is no direction, no point, no hope. For some of you, life without God and His guidance might be fine. You have the education, the job, the money, and some respect. You have the American dream. Your scars might be hidden. Or you have learned to live with or ignore them. I hear you. I get you.

Respectfully, I say, honey, you are being played. You are being deceived and lied to. You are depending on stuff that you can lose in a heartbeat. Age, illness, cultural upheavals, and economic down-turns—a pandemic—can disrupt or rob us of our man-made dreams and goals.

Such is life.

Yet God is the One who can breathe life into the dead, resurrect buried dreams, and offer hope to those who have lost everything. He soothes our wounded souls, minds, and bodies. He bathes our scars with His own scarred hands and accepts us as we are. God does amazing things. When things are at their bleakest, He shows up.

You want proof? Keep reading.

### "Look at Mine"

By Denise Ann Goosby

I walk into a room and the looks begin—
A glance from her, a stare from him.
A childish giggle echoes from behind me,
And once again I walk straight ahead.

A familiar pain awakens me to darkness.
My body longs for peace and rest.
But I know neither will come tonight,
And I'm left disappointed on my bed.

I cast my cares upon You, Lord.
It's what my heart knows it should do.
But it's hard to speak my hurt and longing
When the cause of all my pain is You.
Lord, why did You make me this way,
With a heart and body so broken and scarred?
I know Your scars are proof of Your love,
But what good can come from mine?

A still small voice meets me in my anger,
Reminding me of what I know is true.
"Let your scars prove your love for Me,
Just as My scars prove My love for you."

Faithful are Your wounds, my Savior Friend—
Nothing done without reason or cause.
Even in the wounding there is healing,
For it draws me ever closer to You.
Help me bear the scars You chose to give me,
Forsaking man's desire and praise.
People may not see any beauty,
But You, Jesus, know and have my heart.
So when hurt and rejection surround me,
And others see what only they can see,
I will remember the scars You still carry.
Trembling, I will bear my scars for Thee.

**Devotion**

**Reflect His Heart**

*As water reflects the face, so one's life reflects the heart.*
Proverbs 27:19

I was wrong to think I could make a life on my own power.

How could I? I was missing the most important part. I thought the responsibility for making a life rested on my shoulders. Life seemed like a series of decisions I had to get right. I had to pick the right school and get the right job and get the right house. I had to order my own steps. Have the wisdom and foresight to make my own way—make my own life. I was trying to do what culture and society told me I should do. And I was doing it without God.

That is no way to make a life.

I made living about me. I made life about my own wins and losses, my successes and my scars. Life was what I saw through my senses. But life is a heart issue. It is about the values and integrity within you expressed through your words and actions. It is being disciplined enough, gentle enough, and loving enough to push past your own great fears and pains to love God and love others.

Like Jesus.

Jesus reflected the heart of God perfectly. God wanted to "make human beings in our image, make them reflecting our nature" (Genesis 1:26 MSG). God desired that we would rule, create, prosper, and love as He does, for the "The LORD, the LORD God, compassionate and gracious, slow to anger, and abounding in lovingkindness and truth (faithfulness)" (Exodus 34:6 AMP). Life is not something you grasp but something you give away extravagantly. Life is about relationship, first with God and then with others.

Jesus says it plainly: "I am the way and the truth and the life" (John 14:6). Life is found in knowing and following God's Word—and if we want to know how to walk through this world, we need to imitate how the God-man Christ lived His life. Jesus came to serve and tell others about God. He went about doing good. He defended women and children and the poor. He spoke the truth. He lived right—with purpose and purity. Jesus only did the will of Father God. Life for Him was not in money, fame, or position. It was not in how much power He could wield. Life for Jesus was showing how much love He could give away.

I want that type of life for you and for me.

But we, with our scars both hidden and visible, cannot make such a life on our own. If we want our lives to reflect God's heart, then we must believe and receive God's Word. His Word says we are sacred spaces where His Spirit lives. Our lives are not our own but God's. There is honor and power when we give our soul-scarred bodies away so God can live through us (1 Corinthians 6:19–20; Galatians 2:20).

We give control to an all-powerful God who gives us "everything we need for a godly life" (2 Peter 1:3) and promises to never leave our side. Now, this faith walk must be learned and relearned. We need to give ourselves grace for our imperfections and scars and healing. We need to give mercy to others for their own shortcomings and wounds and recovery. It is hard work. But it is worth it.

You are worth it.

## Questions to Ponder in Your Heart
How is God a part of your life?
How is God not a part of your life?
What are the best and worst parts of your life?
What part(s) of your life do you need to surrender and commit to prayer?

## Prayer
*Father God, You have always known me.* You made me in Your image, and Your desire is that my heart reflect Your heart. Father, do Your

work in me. Show me how to love You and the people around me. Help me to honor You with the body I have knowing You will make Your strength perfect in my weakness. You will bring beauty—Your beauty—to my life. To You be the glory. Amen.

**Memory Verses**

> You make known to me the path of life; you will fill me with joy in your presence with eternal pleasures at your right hand. (Psalm 16:11)

> This is my comfort in my affliction, that your promise gives me life. (Psalm 119:50 ESV)

# Chapter 5

# WHERE DO I BELONG?

*If we live, we live for the Lord; and if we die, we die for the LORD. So, whether we live or die, we belong to the LORD.*
Romans 14:8

"*This room is always freezing.*" I sighed ruefully.

The cold hit me as soon as I opened the door. I could see my dad slightly hunched over in a chair. He offered me a slight smile and leaned back. I slowly ambled over to him, quickly giving a smile to the older Filipino gentleman who sat nearby. He and my dad had formed a silent bond in the days they had spent together in this hospital waiting for their wives to heal. Sitting beside my dad, I took a deep breath.

It had been several days since Mom was taken by ambulance from my house to Gardena Memorial. Mom had come to my place to recover after another hospital stay. But she grew dehydrated. The family was concerned, but we assumed Mom would respond to fluids and more treatment and return to us.

A few days later, I went to visit Mom after work and ran into my dad.

"Your mom loved you very much," my dad said softly, choking up as he said the words. I caught my breath. He explained that Mom had taken a turn for the worse. Her heart, which the doctors had warned needed surgery years before, was now failing. She had been moved into the tiny ICU across the hall and put on a ventilator. Helpless, I rubbed my sister's shoulder as we watched the nurses work to remove the fluid from Mom's lungs. Sometimes they frowned at us and Dad when we came to visit. "Too many people," they said. One Saturday night, Mom's heart fluttered before the staff got her stabilized. I looked up to see one of the nurses walking toward me, silently holding a chair that she placed beside Mom's bed. Quietly, I sat down to be with my mom.

Now, Monday, I had returned to the hospital to join my dad while my sister was at dialysis. I admired my dad's strength, but I also felt sorry for him. The summer before, his mother had died at ninety-two. Dad had spent years visiting her and bringing food to her convalescent room. That was in addition to watching over Mom and helping my sister with her health issues. After his mother passed, Dad blamed himself for not being more attentive to her care.

And here he was again with my mom.

I guess that is what love looks like.

The little gentleman said his goodbyes and left the room, leaving Dad and me alone. A sound by the door alerted us. We looked up to see a man carrying a tool pouch. He headed straight to the thermostat. After a few minutes, a bit of warmth began to flood the room. Then suddenly, I knew I would never visit the room again.

"How ironic," I mused quietly.

A few minutes later, I heard, "Code blue! Code blue!"

I knew it was my mom.

I looked at my dad. He seemed lost in his own thoughts. I wondered, *How long before they tell us?* I stilled myself for what was coming. A few minutes later, a white-coated physician walked in and spoke to my dad. Mom was gone. "She is?" he asked with surprise in his voice. "I thought she would pull through." Such faith. Dad believed God could do anything. Dad had seen God work miraculously many times. His own life of hardship, healing, deliverance, and God's grace proved it. Yet God's ways are not our ways. And what He gives, He can take away.

Things had to be done. I called my school, letting the phone ring and ring until my principal, Miss Jeffries, answered. I told her my mom had just died and that I would not be at work for a while. Shocked, she asked what she could do and offered to contact a few of my colleagues. Her concern lifted a burden from my shoulders. Then I called my cousin Trish. Her mother was a younger sister of my mom. We had grown up together. Our families lived next door as neighbors for twenty-five years. She was closer to my sister than I was.

"I need you to come and help me tell Lanthe," I said.

"Okay," she replied through tears. I could hear her crying as I hung up. A few minutes later, Dad and I walked out of the hospital. The gentleman whose wife was also in the hospital met us and expressed his apologies. I wondered if he would lose his wife too.

"I guess I'll have to go into a convalescent home now until I die too," my dad said half-jokingly to me as we walked through the parking lot.

"No, Dad. You are not going to a home. I want you to come and live with me," I said firmly. Having him live by himself in that house with all its stuff and memories did not sit well with me. I wanted my dad safe and close to me. Lanthe had already lived with me for several months. She came after spending three months in the hospital after a severe flare up of her lupus.

With Mom dead, I wanted the three of us together.

Dad was conflicted. He and Mom had been married for forty-four years. Had lived in the same house for more than forty. He had lived through Mom's voices and illnesses and all the trials that married people go through. His had been a hard marriage. Yet it was even harder for him to say goodbye. "I miss you," Dad greeted his empty house after Mom passed. Even so, Dad gathered up some of his belongings and returned that night to my place.

By that time, Trish had arrived with a family friend to help me break the news to my sister. She was heartbroken. We were heartbroken for her. Her grief was so visceral—so physical—I worried she would end up in the hospital herself. She eventually grew calmer, especially when Dad came and moved into the room Mom had stayed in.

Dad had a funeral service for Mom a week later at Rose Hills Memorial Park in Whittier. It was in an older area of the property inside a small circle-shaped chapel. I was thankful for the family, neighbors, and people from my school who came to support us and to honor my mom. Mom had isolated herself, so she had no friends of her own.

For many years, I hated the pain my mom caused our family. I hated hearing the voices. I hated it when she said I could not have playmates or when she grew angry and hit me. I hated all the stuff that filled our house. I hated the ugly words she spoke to me or Dad. But when I became a Christian, she was the first one I talked to about God. I wanted her to know Jesus. I wanted her life to belong to Him. I wanted her to live with Him in heaven forever. I wondered if my words had penetrated her mind and if she was able to understand her need for Christ despite her mental illness. I know she said the prayer to receive Him.

It would have to be enough.

I did not want to be like my mother.

I did not want to be without friends—people I could talk to and do things with. I decided I would join the singles ministry at my church. They met in a smaller room on Friday nights. People would gather to mingle, snack, and talk. Then service always began with a worship band before the singles pastor gave a message, and the evening ended in prayer and more talking. Often the group would migrate en masse to a restaurant down the street.

The pastor was well-liked and dynamic and had a servant team that helped him and his wife organize events. One week we would deliver food baskets for families of a local boys and girls club. The next week we could be helping with the church's harvest festival. Another week we could be singing Christmas carols or handing out gospel tracts on the pier. There was always something to do. I loved that our group was busy and that we had fun and that we helped people. I eventually transitioned from volunteering with the children's ministry after I was asked to join the servant team.

I was finding a place to belong.

During this time, God began to reintroduce singing and writing back into my life. I wrote devotionals for the singles website and helped to write a play that our group put on for our singles gathering. I began to fantasize about being a Christian journalist who would travel the world reporting and writing stories for Christian publications. Maybe my dream of being Nancy Drew with a pen was not dead but reimagined.

Instead God used an auburn-haired Kansas girl to redirect my path into worship music. One day Mendy and I met after Sunday service. How or why, I do not recall. Mendy played piano and sang for the praise team. As it turned out, she also gave vocal lessons out of her apartment. I was intrigued. Singing had brought me so much joy as a little girl. But I had not done any singing since my high school glee club days. The last time I even wanted to sing was for a talent show in the tenth grade. I had planned to audition for my teacher before class one day and had showed up after the bell rang. "I don't think you want to do this," she said as she watched me come through the door. I mumbled something and quickly left before starting to cry.

Now, years later, I had Jesus. He would give me the courage to sing again. I looked for Mendy at church. She had disappeared. For months I did not see or hear anything about her until she came up to me while I was gathering my belongings after a late service one Sunday. I was stunned but happy to see her. Mendy remembered our earlier talk about singing. We agreed to meet at her apartment for a lesson the next day.

"Hi, how you doing?" Mendy greeted me at the gate. "I'm okay," breathless and thankful that I had found the right place. I saw the piano as soon as I walked through the door. After settling in, we talked about how she would help me. She asked me what I wanted to sing.

"You are my hiding place, You always fill my heart . . ." were the words that came out of my mouth.

For the next thirty minutes, Mendy played and I sang. Sometimes she harmonized with me. She said I sounded like an alto who could sing high. I think that was a good thing. She asked if I wanted to continue with the lessons. "Sure," I said, real cool like. Later, as I got back into the car, I had to let it out. "God, that was so much fun!" I shouted, banging the steering wheel with my right hand. The second-century Christian theologian Irenaeus said that the glory of God is man fully alive.

Baby, I was alive and I wanted more.

After several months of lessons, the idea of singing worship for the singles ministry grew in my spirit. By then, a new pastor was overseeing our group. Like Mendy, he was also a member of the church praise band. He would have high expectations. I made an appointment to audition with him. When I heard the first chords of his guitar, I smiled inside. I started to sing, and he joined me in harmony.

The next Friday found me rehearsing with our singles band—if you could call it that. It is hard to sing when you cannot breathe, and the huge pit in my stomach felt overwhelming. Suddenly, I was in high school again, teary-eyed as I watched the kids participating in the talent show I should have been in. I fled for the hallway after practice.

People were gathering for the service. Soon it would start and probably without me. The only thing alive at that moment was my fear. I wanted to run. The only reason I decided to sing that night was because I was afraid that God would take away my ability to sing—my talent—and give it to someone who would use it.

So I sang. I did it afraid. And it was hard and terrifying . . . and glorious. The next time I sang, the anxiety remained, but it was less intense and not as overwhelming. It seemed that whenever I opened my mouth, God would fill it (Psalm 81:10). Within a year, Mendy and I were doing worship house concerts. Sometimes I would read the devotionals I had written before I sang. During a mission trip to Scotland, my friend Lester played the guitar, and I joined him on vocals as we ministered in parks, on street corners, and at a local mall. I even shared my writings and songs for singles events.

One night during our church's special time of prayer for the sick and hurting, Lester and I sang praise and worship while people prayed for and anointed people with oil. A family came in with a child who was unresponsive. But once the music began, he moved. When I heard that, I knew I was put on this earth for a reason. I just knew. And I wanted to be a part of healing others through music.

Mendy and I had tentatively named the budding ministry Cup of Praise. Worship had expanded my world. It expanded my possibilities to minister and use my gifts. I looked forward to what God would do in my life.

However, my sense of belonging felt tenuous.

Even though I was forging ties and relationships with the people around me, I was still conscious of my keloids, especially the one that formed on my face after I got the chicken pox in grad school. It was hard for me to look in the mirror. It was hard for me to see myself as worthy of someone's time and affection. I felt ugly unless I was singing and doing it well.

I remembered what an older sister in Christ had said to me during an earlier mission trip to Russia. We were in our dorm room talking about our hopes for the future. I talked about how I wanted to be married and to have someone who would look beyond my scars and the size of my body and to love me for me.

"Maybe God doesn't want to share you," she said, not unkindly.

Maybe He doesn't want to share me? Hmm. Okay. I nervously laughed off the comment. How could I not? The alternative would be to share how hurt and afraid the words made me feel. The alternative would be to acknowledge that she might be right. The alternative would be to rethink what I believed—that God would lead me to a man who would marry me.

Was it too much to hope that God would give me someone to belong to?

"My mom died, Nicey. I just heard them code her over the phone." My heart dropped as I took in what my cousin had told me. Aunt Cora was dead. The one whose home I ran to as a refuge from my mother's voices. The one who did my hair and took me shopping because my mom couldn't. The one who enrolled me in Catholic school. She was dead. Silent, I listened as Trish explained that there were issues with the burial insurance and that she needed help to fund and plan a funeral. I remembered how my dad was after Mom died. He was wooden, barely able to think or move.

"It's okay. I can help," I said with more certainty than I felt.

I made plans to visit her so we could discuss what arrangements needed to be made. When I told my dad about the death, he offered to give her a spare burial site that he had at Rose Hills. Dad, being Dad, had bought extra plots for our family after his mother died. The one he gave my cousin for her mom was next to my mother, Anna. That meant she and Aunt Cora would be side by side, just as they were when they were neighbors. That seemed fitting. It also meant that Dad would no longer have a plot.

"I'll probably be buried in Riverside," Dad replied, referring to the military cemetery sixty miles to the east. Dad had served in the army during the Korean War. My mother's brother, Willie, also an army veteran, was buried at Riverside.

Things seemed to be coming together. I had just received my tax refund too, and it was enough to pay for a funeral. The problem was that the money was to fund a mission trip to China I was set to take four months later in July. And unbeknownst to Trish and my dad, I desperately needed to take that trip.

My heart was broken.

I thought God had done it—that He had brought a man into my life who would love and care for me. Scriptures had come that

I believed confirmed it, and we grew closer. Eventually, he joined the singles group and became a part of the ministry. He played for the worship band. We were always doing things together. He even mailed me a little note in appreciation of our friendship. But a few weeks before Christmas, he called me. He wanted my advice and help. A woman had captivated his heart. It wasn't me. He wanted to know what to do. "I just want to bless her," he said.

It would have been hilarious if it had not hurt so much. Somehow I got through the call. I spoke encouraging words to him. I built him up. I pointed him to God and His will for him . . . and for her. That's what you do for those you love. After a few minutes, we said our goodbyes, and I hung up. "Why did You do this? Why did You let this happen?" I screamed to the ceiling, balling my fists and collapsing on my bed. I could scarcely bear the pain. Betrayal. Gut punching betrayal. God had rewarded my faith with betrayal. I felt betrayed and disappointed in God. I could not fathom what had happened. Who was this God who had broken my heart seemingly beyond repair?

Then the phone rang. I answered and talked. I hung up. It rang again. I answered and talked. I hung up. It rang again. I answered and talked. I hung up. It rang again. Six or seven times it rang—each time with a sister or brother in Christ checking in to see how I was doing. None of them knew about what happened. Cute. Sweet even. But I wasn't in the mood. After the last ring, I had had enough.

"You can stop the calling now!" I snapped at the ceiling.

Spent, I sighed and grew still, looking around the room. I wasn't so much searching for something—I just wanted to know what to do next. All my beliefs and suppositions about what I believed to be true were in question. It was more than just having my heart broken. My pain, my disappointment with my circumstances, and my dashed and deferred hope—my inner scars—now marred how I saw God. They validated my lifelong fear of Him. This God who said He loves me had chosen not to act in the way I expected and wanted Him to. This God who said I am His child and that I belong to Him. This God who said nothing is impossible for Him. This God who created the heavens and earth and holds back wind and waves.

"Yours is a hard love, God," I mused, shaking my head. A hard love.

My friend asked his lady to marry him Valentine's night. I was there. It was at our usual Friday night singles gathering. Earlier that week, he had said he would call me to share something with me. In fact, he had said he would call Valentine's Day. So I waited. He never called. That night before we began worship practice, I watched him, thinking he might say something.

"I waited for your call," I said when he stopped in front of me. His answer was to look down. Then he said, "I know, Denise." He reached out and gave me a brotherly rub on my shoulder. My left shoulder—the one with the keloid scarring. His hand stilled and his eyes widened in shock as he felt the scarring. Then he caught himself, softened his touch, and looked at me before turning away.

"Congratulations!" one of our friends said to him a few minutes later. Puzzled, I looked back and forth between the two of them.

"You didn't hear? He's an engaged man today."

"Oh."

The man I thought God had given me was now engaged to another woman.

Yeah. Hard love. Hard love.

I had believed and desperately wanted to believe, even after he told me he wanted to bless her. Well, it did not matter what I thought. I just had to go on. But it was hard to go on. In fact, after a few months I was depressed with suicidal thoughts. I felt rejected by people and by God. My keloids were getting worse. The infection and ulceration became almost continuous, robbing me of sleep at night and energy for my days. My anger at God often simmered below the surface, only to burst out in fits of crying and screaming that I made sure no one witnessed. Except for Mendy, no one knew how I felt.

*Why did You even let me be born? Why couldn't I have died like all the babies my mom miscarried before me?*

My words did not seem to move God.

But I knew something had to change. Quite simply, I needed a reason to live. I needed a purpose to motivate me to reengage with life again. One day I received some information from the Christian aid and development organization Food for the Hungry. I had requested information about them months ago when I went to a Christmas concert featuring John Tesh and Nicole C. Mullen. They had a short-term mission trip to China scheduled for mid-July. They needed people to teach English as a second language to middle school students for several days. Team members would stay in a hotel across the street from the school. There would be other activities too. *This could bring purpose back into my life,* I decided silently. Perhaps I could find healing and belonging in doing God's work.

I filled out the paperwork and was accepted onto the team several weeks later. I started planning. I read and reread all the forms and booklets Food for the Hungry sent me. I viewed their website and examined all the articles and pictures. Whenever I travel to a new place, I always purchase a guidebook. Online information is great, but when I hold the book in my hand and open it to read, my trip becomes real in my mind.

Only this time, I felt numb when I picked up one on China. I wasn't sure why, except that nothing much moved me lately. I felt as if I had just been going through the motions of living. I guess it was enough that I was going—so I hoped. But with the money allocated for my aunt's funeral, the trip looked unlikely.

That meant I needed to concentrate more on my class at school. Because my kindergartners were second-language learners, I had to take a Thursday night Spanish course for teachers offered by my district. Learning more of the language would help me better communicate with my kids. It was also good that they saw me as a student too. I often told them that I would teach them English, and they would teach me Spanish.

I was not a good student. After several years in the classroom, I probably could put together five or ten sentences in Spanish. I was thankful to have had some wonderful bilingual aides who worked with me as I taught. Yes, for a lot of reasons, attending the class would be helpful. But I was not looking forward to the drive. The three-hour class was in Venice—forty-five minutes away from work. Then I had another hour drive to my home in Compton.

Once I got there, I enjoyed the class. The instructor was a lovely teacher who used pictures, real-world conversations, and novellas (Spanish dramas) to teach us the language. It occurred to me to ask her to translate some of the worship songs I sang in church into Spanish. She was kind enough to help me. I did not know why or how I would use the songs.

Soon I got a call from my cousin Trish. She and the insurance company had resolved the issues with her mother's life insurance. The company paid her money for her claim, and she was able to pay me back. I had the money I needed for the trip.

"I really need to be learning Chinese," I mumbled to myself during Spanish class one night. When class ended, I untangled myself from my desk and walked as quickly to the car as my fluffy body allowed me. After driving for several minutes, my stomach tightened. Tension seeped into my muscles, and I blinked as headlights continuously flashed in front of me. Then the fear hit. I hurried to roll down my window, trying to get air and to keep myself from passing out.

*Oh, God, help me!* I prayed silently, then out loud.

It was happening again.

Off and on for several years, I had suffered with episodes of anxiety when I drove, especially at night. I never understood what caused them and never even thought to see a doctor. They would last for a couple of minutes. Sometimes they would stop on their own or after I reached my destination. I could go months or years without experiencing them.

But a few weeks into my Spanish class, the old sensations reappeared on my drive home. And they grew worse throughout the duration of the class. Thankfully, I am not a freeway driver, so speed was not an issue. But if you have ever had to travel by streets in a large city, you know how time consuming and frustrating it can be. Add a panic attack on top of that, and you have a disaster in the making. But God got me home, shaken and sometimes close to tears, but home and safe. I was thankful, especially when I finished my last Spanish class and drove home and parked in my garage with a smile on my face.

I did more than finish a course or a scary drive. In my spirit, something broke free. I could continue to prepare for China and for the students for whom I would be teaching English. China was in the news a lot. Reporters spoke about a new virus called SARS that began to circulate. It had sickened and killed many Chinese. The virus alarmed people all over the world. Even officials in the United States sought information, determined to keep the virus from infecting Americans.

Food for the Hungry was concerned too. They had people in China monitoring the situation. SARS had infected people in a providence adjacent to the one our team would be serving. We were due to leave in two months. Our final payment for the trip would need to go out soon. After a few more weeks, a decision was made to cancel the trip to China and redirect our team to another place. Good work was being done in Eastern Europe and Latin America, noted a letter I got about where our group might go. The new trip would be in August. They would find a new project for us.

Funny. Once Food for the Hungry pulled us out of China, I stopped hearing about SARS and China. Apparently, the virus had either run its course or cures were found. It was no longer in the news. It just disappeared.

At first it looked like our group would go to Columbia. But that meant the person who would be leading us would also be shepherding several mission teams, and he would be overwhelmed. Romania was their next choice. That sounded interesting. But the trip would have been for a month, and I had to start fall semester the end of August.

Guatemala was the place Food for the Hungry finally decided to send us. Intrigued, I purchased a guidebook to Guatemala. The colorful pictures of native dress, marketplaces, and city buses pulled at my spirit. I was captivated by the little villages, fifteenth-century towns with cobble-stoned streets, large cities sprawling across acres of land, and volcanoes towering over them all off in the distance.

I enjoyed reading about the Garifuna people, a mixed Afro-Caribbean and native population who migrated from the island of Saint Vincent to the Central American coastlands. I wondered if I would get to see them. Guatemala is known as the "place of the eternal spring." It made me chuckle that I was leaving California, the "land of the endless summer," for the "place of the eternal spring."

"Oh, Denise, you don't want to go there. Can't you go someplace else?" my friend E said to me nervously over the phone.

My mirth quickly turned to foreboding. Guatemala had suffered a decades-long civil war between its established government and anti-government rebels. Thousands of civilians had died or disappeared over the years because of the fighting. Thousands of others fled the country to other areas. Many settled in Southern California, home to the largest Central American populace outside the region. I checked out the United States Department of State website. It warned potential travelers to be careful. Political tensions remained. It was an election year in Guatemala. Poverty was widespread, and crime was a common occurrence in the capital of Guatemala City. After reading the article from the State Department, I took a deep breath. I did not sign up for this. I just wanted a reason to get up in the morning. I wanted to soothe my broken heart by helping others. Now it seemed I had led myself into danger.

I had to go through with it. I had given my word and paid my money. And I was needed. Our original group of sixteen men and women had been reduced to about half—all women, except for one young man who got engaged to one of the members a week before the trip. Our project was to travel high into the mountains to help build public school classrooms for the Xitchil people in the morning and hold a vacation Bible school (VBS) in the afternoon. Our group leader had her hands full and needed someone to teach the VBS classes. Since I was a teacher, it seemed the natural thing for me to do. My construction skills rendered me useless anyway.

I read up online about the trip a few days before we were scheduled to leave. Guatemala's Fuego Volcano had erupted a week or two before. The volcano was located near Antigua, a beautiful European-style city where our team would spend a day or two during our eight-day trip.

*Lord in heaven, volcanoes are erupting,* I thought. *Nothing is safe about this trip.* Glancing at the living room window next to me, I shut off the computer and headed for my bedroom. I should have been on my way to church. My dad had left for service ten minutes ago. But my heart was not in it, so I decided to stay home. As I entered the hallway, I vaguely heard the sound of idling cars in traffic.

The first boom took my breath away. I whirled around as more booms sounded around me. I thought they were coming right at me. Gun shots. Big. Heavy. Malevolent. And lethal. When they ended, I peeked around the corner into the living room, shocked not to see bullets and debris littering the floor. Walking to the window, I cautiously looked out. Neighbors gathered on the corner near my house. Cars were slowly starting to move. I opened the door and went outside, praying silently as I did. Then I stopped. To my left, I saw a motorcycle and a body lying in the street. The poor man never had a chance. One of the neighbors said she looked out her window and saw him move slightly before going still. Hearing that made the encounter even more chilling for me.

"You wouldn't kill a dog that way," my dad said when he came home later that night. His words unnerved me, but I was thankful to see him. The sheriffs had closed off our street to investigate. I worried how he and my sister, who was visiting some of our relatives, would get home, but they eventually both made it home safely.

I could not shake the irony.

Here I was worried about going to Guatemala with its hardship, crime, volcanoes, and uncertainty. Yet violence had happened right outside my front door. I sensed God speak to me: *I protected you here. I will protect you there.*

God was true to His word.

He got me through the airport maze of checkpoints and boarding gates, depositing my teammates and me safely in Guatemala City. The officials who greeted us deemed the capital too dangerous for us to stay. They immediately took us to a Lutheran compound a half an hour away. We stayed there overnight. In the morning, we made a five- or six-hour van ride across a valley and then up into the mountains. The trip took us through small cities and towns. I marveled at the bright colors painted on all the buses and worn by the people. Our young guide, Mr. Lee, regaled us with stories and facts about the culture and politics of Guatemala. He told us about the village in which we would do our building and outreach. Our ride ended when we pulled aside a tiny hotel tucked amid a quiet neighborhood not far from the local offices for Food for the Hungry. I grew to enjoy the humble little place with its modest rooms. The owners were a family who emigrated from Spain. They were kind, considerate, and good cooks. They almost made up for the cold shower, bathroom doors that locked on their own, and the spiders I chased out of my bed.

The next morning, our team met up with two teenage boys who bravely came to Guatemala on their own to do missions work. They were staying a few blocks away from us. I was concerned for them and for all of us really. I had seen the number "18" markings on some of the buildings around us. It was the tag of a well-known gang in Los Angeles. They were so violent that LAPD went to a judge to put special sanctions on them. Now they were in Guatemala—six thousand feet up in the mountains. Yet the locals treated their presence as ordinary. Our team was there to minister, and that's what we did.

Every day for five days, we walked ten minutes to the Food for the Hungry field office. We gathered supplies, food, and people and we squeezed into as many cars and trucks as we could find. Then we meandered through the village traffic out to the countryside. We occasionally picked up one or two or even three more people. An hour later, we arrived at the main Xitchil hamlet of tiny wooden stores, huts, buildings, and school rooms.

About thirty or forty children stopped what they were doing and came to meet us. They were an excitable bunch—too much.

"Denise, help!" one of my teammates yelled as a crowd of happy children surrounded us.

It seemed a good time to be a teacher. After corralling the maddening crowd, we sat down to draw pictures, sing songs, and tell stories. Praise God for strength and crayons. A few of the teachers came looking for their students. We exchanged greetings. One invited me to visit his class. It was a total God moment. I got to teach them an English lesson and sing praise songs to them in Spanish. Such became most of my mornings for the week.

In the afternoon, I taught a VBS class while my teammates took a break from constructing classrooms to do crafts or play sports with the children. I wanted to show the children how God values families and that He longs for them to be a part of His family. I used the story of Abraham and his son Isaac as an example. The first time I talked with the students in class, I was disappointed by the silence and stoic faces that confronted me.

After a few days of the same reaction—or lack of reaction—I felt discouraged. A Guatemalan Christian encouraged me. She said it was a sign of respect for the students to be still and quiet. One day one of the older students said something to the interpreter who was helping me. She said she appreciated what I was teaching her class. I looked at the shy twelve-year-old who refused to make eye contact with me. *Okay, Lord. I am doing some good here.*

God was the One at work in Guatemala.

He was the One who allowed a Christian organization to come and help build classrooms for a public school. God was the One who gave the team the skill, toughness, and tenacity to become temporary construction workers. When the Xitchil saw this group of women working on their behalf, it inspired some of the men to join the effort. It also opened the door for their women to do construction work too. More importantly, God moved the hearts of many young people who raised their hands on the last day of VBS to become a part of God's forever family. Our team and the locals shared tears of joy amid all the happy smiles.

Our mission trip guide, Mr. Lee, looked at me. I knew he wanted me to speak to the assembled group of parents, students, and team members. Our group was packing up to drive back to the field office for the last time. Tomorrow we would drive to Antigua, shop at the marketplace, and spend the night at the Lutheran compound. Then we would be up before dawn, racing through the streets of Guatemala City with a decoy shadowing us, before catching an early morning flight back to America. After hesitating, I thanked them for letting me teach the children.

Later that night at the hotel, the team and some of the local officials of Food for the Hungry met to celebrate. We talked about our experiences, laughed, and prayed. Mr. Lee said God had protected us. He told us that when we were driving up the narrow mountain roads, he feared we were about to be robbed. Some cars had blocked our way briefly, which was a typical maneuver of bandits.

I laughed when I remembered meeting Mr. Lee's grandmother while running an errand one day. He was a light-skinned Guatemalan with European and not native blood. I wondered why his name was Lee. Then I saw him hug his grandmother . . . a full-blooded Chinese woman. Like some of the Chinese in California and Mexico, people from China in search of jobs also migrated to Guatemala. Ah, yes, God does have a sense of humor.

One of the men recounted to us how the mission team that usually came to help the Xitchil were not able to come that year. They knew they had to get those classrooms built. They prayed and waited. And our team came. We had not been what they expected. But God had answered and did above and beyond what was asked or imagined (Ephesians 3:20). I was impressed.

"These people prayed us up out of China and brought us here," I said in amazement.

God rolls that way.

When we least expect it.

When we're not even looking for it.

When we're angry and upset and thoroughly discouraged, convinced God has failed or abandoned us, He shows up, shows out, and does something ridiculously wonderful. God cannot help but be Himself. God cannot help but be awesome. God cannot help but be faithful and gracious and compassionate. Who is God? I'm glad you asked.

He is Elohim, the creator God—the maker of everything and everyone.

He is Jehovah, the Eternal One—the God who was and is and forever will be.

He is Yahweh, the all-existent One—the God who calls things into being.

He is El Shaddai, the mighty God—the God of heaven.

He is Jesus Christ, the anointed One—the messianic God who saves and delivers us.

That is God.

He is the God who says to us: You already belong to Me.

Do not fear, for I have redeemed you; I have summoned you by name; you are mine. (Isaiah 43:1)

We belong to God.

We have an everlasting tie that binds us to Him. Nothing and no one can sever our relationship with Him. Nothing can snatch us out of the hands of the Father. Intellectually, we get this. In our hearts, not so much. We pursue people and things and status and beauty in the natural when God has already given all of it to us by His Spirit.

And not only you, but anyone who sacrifices home, family, fields—whatever—because of me will get it all back a hundred times over, not to mention the considerable bonus of eternal life. This is the Great Reversal: many of the first ending up last, and the last first. (Matthew 19:29–30 MSG)

By God's grace, we will hold on until that *Great Reversal*.

What about my pain? What about my scars? I am not going to kid you. I have no sure answer as to why this perfect, powerful, miracle-working God of love would let His people suffer heartbreak, physical affliction, hurt, and loss. I just know that He does. I also know that God cannot lie.

He tells us throughout His Scriptures that we will have tribulation. We will face dark valleys, perplexing situations, and enemies from within and around us. We will have our hopes dashed and our dreams deferred. We will make mistakes. We will sin and be sinned against. Life just rolls that way. But as the old gospel song "Because He Lives" tells us, life is worth the living because our God lives.

> The LORD your God is with you, the Mighty Warrior who saves. He will take great delight in you; in his love he will no longer rebuke you, but will rejoice over you with singing. (Zephaniah 3:17)

God has engaged Himself to us as a man does to a woman. He pledges to us His presence, provision, protection, and power. He promises that if we fall, He will pick us up. If we go through tough times, He will scatter treasure in the midst for us to find. Others may reject us—may back away from the scars we carry—but God accepts us into His beloved family.

With God, we will always find a place to belong.

### "God's Time"
By Denise Ann Goosby

The ticking of the clock,
The passing of the days,
The sand within the hour glass—
How I long to know Your ways.

You say that those who wait for You
Will be amazed at what You do.
It's the hope I have in Your faithfulness
That keeps my eyes on You.

Time has a way of humbling us
When nothing else will do.
We're forced to trust Your Word, Oh God,
Put our confidence in You.

Still I fight the fear inside
That Your Word for me won't stand.
That I'll be disappointed—
See my dreams slip through my hands.

God's time is not my time.
God's time is not my time.
God's time is not my time,
But it's still beautiful.
Not a single promise You have made
Will ever die or fail.
You're a Gentleman who keeps His word,
Through it all, Your plans prevail.

So I'll fight the fear inside
That Your word for me won't stand,
And I won't be disappointed
As I hold those dreams in my hands.

God's time is not my time.
God's time is not my time.
God's time is not my time,
But it's still beautiful. [Repeat]

All will be well.
All will be beautiful.
I will put my hope in You. [Tag]

God's time is not my time,
But it's still beautiful.

© Denise Ann Goosby 2020

## Devotion

### A Taste from the Well

*Everyone who drinks from this water will be thirsty again; but
whoever drinks of the water that I will give him shall never be thirsty;
but the water that I give him will become in him a fountain of water
springing up to eternal life.*
John 4:13–14 NASB

All I wanted was to have friends and a man who would love me for
me—someone who would see the beauty in my scars. That is what
I was searching for the first night I walked into my church's singles
ministry. I figured if there were a safe place for me and my wounds
and issues, this was it.

Have you been there?

Have you waited anxiously for your classmates to pick you for
dodgeball?

Have you wondered if your acting was good enough for the
school play?

Have you prayed that this date or this encounter would lead you
to your soul mate?

Have you wanted to be wanted?

We all want to belong to someone. We all want to be chosen and
to be deemed worthy. God Himself said it was not good for Adam
to be alone. So He made Eve (Genesis 2:18). In Psalm 68:6 it says,
"God sets the lonely in families." Scripture implores us to seek time
with others who follow Christ. And Jesus calls us to let our light shine
before all people that God's goodness might be shown.

But we already belong to Someone.

He calls us beloved, adopted, and chosen. This lover does not play. He inscribed us on His hand and captures our tears in a bottle (Isaiah 49:16; Psalm 56:8). He tells us straight out that He is jealous for us (Exodus 34:14). He says we must love Him with all our heart, soul, mind, and strength (Mark 12:30). He says for us to seek Him passionately and to never forget that He is our first love. Until we abandon ourselves to God's heart for us, we will never be able to love others.

We love him, because He first loved us. (1 John 4:19 KJV)

I know. I hear you. I want the friends and the man too. I want to be accepted by others. Yes, we do. That does not have to cause us shame or guilt or worry about our longings and desires. But we need to focus on God and what He wants from us.

Psalm 37:4 says God will give us our desires. Those longings He will fulfill when His appointed time comes and in the way He deems best. We need to want what He wants. Above all, we need to want Him. If we replace God with anything or anyone else, we will always be the lesser for it. This truth has been part of my story with God. I want to spare you the frustration and ache that comes from putting things and people before God, which is why I wrote about it. I do not want you to unnecessarily add to the scars you already have. Learn from me.

Taste frequently of the sweet, life-giving water God gives through the Bible, prayer, praise, and service. Ask God to show you His plans and purposes for your life—especially about the people you hope to do life with. He knows your heart.

He will care for it.

### Questions to Ponder in Your Heart
What does your heart long for now?
If God met that desire, how would it change your life?
How can you keep God in first place in your life right now?

### Prayer
*Father God, thank You for being my God.* I am so grateful that I belong to You. Thank You for accepting me and my scars. Father, my heart

is the most precious thing I have. Your Word says that all the issues of my life spring from it. Yet my heart has been broken—again and again. Frankly, I wonder if it has ever been whole. Even so, it is a heart that You love. Dear God, please do a new thing in me. Create in me a clean heart that loves You with absolute abandon. Help me to be surrendered to You. Thank You, God. Amen.

**Memory Verse**

> For I am certain that nothing can separate us from his love: neither death nor life, neither angels nor other heavenly rulers or powers, neither the present nor the future, neither the world above nor the world below—there is nothing in all creation that will ever be able to separate us from the love of God which is ours through Christ Jesus our LORD. (Romans 8:38–39 GNT)

# Chapter 6

# WHY AM I IN THE VALLEY

*The hand of the LORD was on me, and he brought me out by the Spirit of the LORD and set me in the middle of a valley; it was full of bones. He led me back and forth among them and I saw a great many bones on the floor of the valley, bones that were very dry. He asked me, "Son of man, can these bones live?" I said, "Sovereign LORD, You alone know."*
Ezekiel 37:1–3

*Sometimes we must go down* before we can go up.

For me that meant following God's will for me and leaving areas that had once brought me joy, recognition, and earthly success for places that were new, hard, and uncertain. First, I left the singles ministry where so much of my discipleship and spiritual maturing had taken place. In the ministry, I used my gifts and talents to proclaim Him. God used the singles group to nurture, refine, and set apart the writing and singing ability He birthed in me during my childhood. He used it to develop new skills, such as planning events and counseling others.

The singles group also launched my appreciation for missions. Whether it was delivering food baskets to needy families in local neighborhoods or helping an orphanage in Peru, I gained a new perspective from the people and places I visited. And all of that was made even more profound because I did it with people who had become a part of my life—people I cared about.

God was stirring change long before He moved me on. My surroundings were changing. People I had known for years were receiving new callings. The pastor who brought me into the singles servant team left to start a church. Two or three more pastors had come and gone. A lot of the people I knew had gotten married. I sang at some of their weddings. I secretly longed to be like them—one of the *successful ones* who found a husband and left our singles ministry to begin life anew. I was thankful for many of the people I met in the group. Yet I felt bereft that I had been denied something my heart longed for. And now I had to leave.

I did not like the new places God was leading me to.

Leaving the singles ministry, I went into the convalescent ministry. A group of us met at church Saturday mornings for worship, devotion, and prayer before splitting up to do services and visitations at nearby assisted living and rehab centers. I had always avoided them. With my parents' and sister's health challenges, I had been in plenty of hospitals and clinics. The smells, the sounds of suffering, and the loneliness I saw in such places frightened me. Death lurked there. I wanted no part of it. But sooner or later, we have to confront our fears. God will have it no other way. He has to break fear's power over us.

The first morning I served in the convalescent ministry, I entered the doors of one center a bit depressed and with a knot in my stomach. I dreaded what I might see and experience. After signing in at the front desk, my small team and I were quietly led to a large, white community room. We gathered at the front of the room and set our things aside. I noted the shuffling of song sheets, purses, and Bibles as we prepared for service.

Glancing around me, I took in the rows of wheelchairs slowly filling the room. A staff member gave water to a white-haired woman sitting quietly nearby. A gentleman with salt-and-pepper hair and folded hands sat quietly by himself. Another woman picked at her robe as she waited for the service to begin. A few residents flashed a brief smile or gave a hello to members of our team they recognized. Most of the people just sat in their chairs staring straight ahead.

Life came into the room as we began to sing the first hymn. Voices—some faint, some strong—joined together and praised God. A few heads nodded. Hands began to move in time with the music. A few smiles lit up faces that a few moments before lacked expression. The familiar and the sacred combined to bring joy to those struggling with pain, sorrow, and longing hearts.

It was lovely to see.

When the songs and teachings ended, our team leader encouraged us to speak with those gathered there. I hesitated. What would I say to them? Then I got over myself and walked forward, saying "thank you" and "God bless you" to the people I greeted. A few times, someone reached out to me, and I gently grasped their hand in mine. No one mentioned my keloids.

When it was time to leave the big room to visit residents who were bedridden, I felt myself wanting to linger. Not wanting to be a hindrance, I joined the team and walked into the hallway. Here we split up, two by two, and happily scattered in all directions. We stopped outside patients' rooms and asked if we could come in. Once invited, we spent a few minutes talking with them, reading Scriptures, praying, and singing songs. It was an uplifting time for all of us. And it was holy. God's presence manifested in the words spoken and the peace that lingered.

My experience at the convalescent home was everything and nothing like I thought it would be. I expected to find pain and suffering and hopelessness. I did. I expected to encounter smells and sounds that unsettled me. I did. I expected to feel afraid, uncertain, and out of place. Yes, I also felt that.

But I also saw love, joy, peace, patience, kindness, goodness, faithfulness, gentleness, and self-control (Galatians 5:22). I saw God's Spirit working in and through the lives of people. I saw God make Himself known to people who many—including me—thought He had forgotten and forsaken. Even with my pride and insensitivity, God desired to use me to serve people He remembered and loved dearly. God gave me what I needed. He humbled me.

This humbling carried over into my work life.

I had been restless for months. I sensed a current of unease running through my spirit. Something was off. My keloids continued to grow worse, which meant I grew more sleep deprived. Getting up and starting work at 7:00 a.m. got harder. Several times I tried to find a teaching position closer to home. But nothing nearby became available. God usually speaks in the stillness. Now in my pain and uncertainty, He was shouting.

And what He was telling me, through the Bible, prayer, and my circumstances, I did not want to hear . . . it was time to resign from my job.

Why on earth would I do that? Teaching for Los Angeles Unified School District (LAUSD) had been a gift. LAUSD helped educate me and allowed me to educate countless children. I had colleagues who had become close friends. I had families who were kind, thoughtful, and appreciative of me as their child's teacher. I fully expected to be like my dad—someone who stays in a job for decades and retires with a pension and the opportunity to enjoy the fruits of labor.

I was like a baby bird too comfortable in its nest. I needed to fly away—from the singles group and from my job. I needed to fly into new, unknown horizons for reasons known only by God. He allowed me to feel unsettled and unfulfilled. Perhaps in my spirit, I knew God wanted to do something new in my life. But I was afraid to let go of the familiar.

It just got too uncomfortable for me to stay where I was.

I found myself speaking to my principal one March morning and announcing my *retirement* to him and the staff. In three months, my time with LAUSD would be over. That meant I had three months to get, fill out, and file all the paperwork I would need to get the money I accrued during my teaching career.

*Regardless, it has to be done.* I sighed.

What would I do with the rest of my life? I was in my early forties. I would have enough money to live on for a little while, but eventually, I would have to look for something. I wondered if God was preparing me to do ministry work.

In recent months, I had researched doing missions work in Israel. Like my dad, I always had a heart for the country and Jewish people. Maybe God was using this transition to move me to Israel. Perhaps I could join a church group or a faith-based organization and help the poor. Maybe I could teach English or establish my own ministry. I wondered what God would do.

God opened the door for me to work with Jewish-loving Christians, not in Israel but in nearby Harbor City. These Christians operated a family run Christian elementary school there. My friend Mendy taught fifth grade at their school. She told me they needed a kindergarten teacher. I hesitated. Teaching and the effects of my keloids had taxed me. Would I feel stronger and healthier working there?

Ultimately, time, prayer, and Bible reading led me to go where I felt God wanted me. He wanted me there. My teaching schedule would be less demanding than with the district. My commute would be easier too. What scared me was that I would make less than a quarter of my salary at LAUSD.

Time and circumstance showed that being a missionary in Israel would not happen—not yet anyway. Maybe teaching at the Christian school would prepare me for the next assignment God had for me. And I could not ignore the timing. The door to public school teaching was closing, and a new one had opened. So when Mendy recommended me to the owners, I visited the school and talked with them. They hired me, and I started teaching during their summer camp a month after separating from LAUSD.

I had to start all over again.

Sometimes it felt like I had never worked in a classroom. I had a new course of study to learn and use with my students. I had a new grade—first grade—an unexpected change that took place when another teacher returned after an illness. There was a different system for requesting and finding materials and supplies. I had to learn how to interact with my colleagues and administrators. I had to get used to being called "Miss Denise" instead of "Miss Goosby."

It was hard for me not to reply in Spanish when little ones asked me a question. Almost all my former students were Latino. Now my class was a rainbow of children with parents who paid to send them to the school and who had high expectations of teachers. Then there was the staring and glances I would get. They saw my keloid scar. It made me feel self-conscious. Different. Out of place.

One day it all became too much for me. I headed for the staff kitchen to sit quietly for a few minutes. A staff member was there talking with her mom who did the cooking. She looked at me. She knew something was wrong.

"I could use a hug," I said, trying not to cry. With understanding, she gathered me in her arms and held me. That embrace helped me to get through the day and the days that followed.

I tried to grasp my new surroundings and the people who filled them. I think God used my new environment and colleagues to chip away at my pride and privilege. I expected life to be a certain way. I expected that I would be a teacher and live a nice, comfortable life. I assumed I would work and interact with the same peers and students who inhabited the world I knew. Even in ministry, I thought I would sing, write, do missions, and serve in the way I always had.

I had built up my identity—again—in the external stuff. How I looked. Where I worked. What I did. I clung to my middle-class life. Yep, I deceived myself. I forgot that I was God's child. I forgot that I belonged to Him and that He called the shots. God had plans and purposes for my life that He fully intended to fulfill. I had to go where He led.

And He had led me to a valley.

I did not want this new life God was giving me. The one I had before was not perfect, but I was comfortable with it. It felt far more secure, fruitful, and satisfying than the shaky one I was trying to navigate.

You know we all want to be a hero. We all want people to think the best of us. But I need to tell on myself before I go any further. I need to clue you in on a choice I made that went against God's will and the consequences it had for me.

Remember the gentleman I thought I was going to marry—the one who broke my heart? Well, it was hard for me to let him go. It was hard to understand how I had missed what God was telling me. I had this desire—this obsession—to know how this man felt about me, especially when he did not call me like he promised. I wrote him a letter asking him how he felt about me, and then I gave him the letter. I am assuming he read it. I say assume because he did not answer me. What he did do was tell a pastor about the letter, which led to me being suspended from ministry for several weeks. Please do not give a married man who is on staff at a church a personal letter. It will not end well.

I was angry at first and then thoroughly ashamed. How could I have done that? It shook me that I could intrude on someone's life and marriage. I would not want someone to do that to me. I had always prided myself on doing the right thing and on being the good girl. I was also burdened with thoughts of being unworthy. *You know what you look like. Why would you think any man would want you?*

The situation was a mess, and I was a mess.

God, thankfully, knows how to clean up a mess. The pastor who initially talked with me was kind and understanding. "We've all acted out of emotion. I have," he said earnestly. I appreciated his honesty and empathy. During my suspension, I had to meet with a women's leader in the church. She was direct. "I can feel the anger in you. It's sad."

That hurt. I really respected her. I did not want to be found wanting in her eyes. But she spoke truth. I could not deny that. The blessing of meeting with her is that she bathed me in words from the Bible. Out of that came a promise in Scripture God gave me, which continues to shape and inform my life:

But you will receive power when the Holy Spirit comes on you, and you will be my witnesses in Jerusalem, and in all Judea and Samaria, and to the ends of the earth. (Acts 1:8)

God had not rejected me.

I may have failed Him, but He did not fail me. He lovingly stayed beside me. He helped me to release my shame and sense of failure—at least enough to move forward—and continue in faith and service.

But scars remained.

These scars were deeper and far more painful than the ones on my body. These wounds validated my fears. They told me I was not worthy of love. They told me people would reject and abandon me, so I better not miss a step. I better do the right thing, say the right thing, and be the right thing. To do less meant I would be found out for the imperfect, broken person I was. I was to learn, though, that there is still beauty in an imperfect, broken person walking through the valley with Jesus.

I learned that lesson through the children at my school—the ones who said I was weird and stared at my scars. Though their behavior and words often made my time in the classroom exhausting and challenging, these children—flaws and all—loved Jesus. They could talk about Him with the accuracy of a trained theologian. The Bible was literal for them. Its stories were not tales written to entertain them. The stories spoke of real people with real issues being broken and imperfect as they walked with God. The children could relate. Their wisdom often left me speechless. They made me envious and humble at the same time. I wanted their pure faith and love for the Lord.

When Mendy asked me to teach and oversee the weekly chapels for the school, I did not feel worthy for the task. I was still trying to regain my confidence as an academic teacher. Now I would be teaching these children about God, about Jesus. I would have to make sure to keep their attention. I should not have worried too much anyway.

I constantly looked for lessons and activities that would make God and the Bible interesting and relevant. Sometimes we used sports competitions, gifts and talent shows, movies and guest speakers. One time we performed a Passover Seder. We put on holiday presentations, had chapels in our mini amphitheater, and did skits and plays. Some of the kids sang for a praise team. I loved that. The best was children's church. The kids did everything, including singing, giving testimonies and sermons, and doing acts of service. It was gratifying to see parents take time from home and work to come and join us. It was even more gratifying to be a part of helping the next generation want to know God and to make Him known.

> How beautiful on the mountains are the feet of those who bring good news, who proclaim peace, who bring good tidings, who proclaim salvation, who say to Zion, "Your God Reigns!" (Isaiah 52:7)

Youth is not wasted on the young. God knows how to stir up gifts and adoration in the hearts of all His people no matter what their season of life. I saw Him work with these students, and I saw Him work with the seniors at the convalescent home.

He was working in and through me too.

Again He nourished my gift of singing. I was asked to join the worship band for the new believers ministry—the one that showed me how to begin living life as a Christian when I was a new believer. Soon our band also became the group for the ministry that served people struggling and recovering from addiction. It made me happy to bring healing and encouragement to them through music.

One Saturday our band performed for our church's harvest celebration. The leader of the group scheduled us after seeing me sing and later asked me to join their ensemble. Again I saw the healing power of music as we sang in prisons, Skid Row missions, and music festivals. I looked forward to what we would do next.

I had also begun singing for a Saturday night Bible study I had started attending three months after I joined the convalescent ministry. The gathering included many people from my church, though the study itself was not affiliated with our congregation. I enjoyed that this group did life together. We often had dinner before our study time. After we sang songs and heard a message, we would talk and share what we experienced that night.

A tight-knit group, we began joining throughout the week for prayer and further study. We often spent weekends and holidays together. We served at outreaches or hosted our own events. We took trips together. We celebrated each other's birthdays. We mourned with and comforted each other in our trials.

A certain gentleman was also a part of this group. I had known him for years. We had mutual acquaintances and had crossed paths in church, with nothing unusual or dramatic. After the fiasco with the earlier person, my heart was still tender. The desire to have someone special in my life remained, but so did the doubt that God would actually do what I believed He had promised me He would.

Everyone knew this gentleman had a lady friend. It was expected that eventually they would marry. I was not going to let myself feel for him. Nope. Been there, done that. Not a good ending. No way did I want to get hurt again. Yet while we were serving together one day, a thought came to me. *This is a man who could love me.*

I watched how he encouraged and accepted people who had physical weaknesses or afflictions. Such a man would not be put off by my scars, my weight, or any other attribute. He could love me for me. But I saw him as, perhaps, a would-be friend—a brother in the Lord. I kept my thoughts about him loving me to myself though.

The kiss near the mouth. The walking me to my car. The chuck under my chin. The invitations to eat with the group, join the Bible study, and sing with the band. It was hard not to think there was something there, especially after I apologized for saying something that hurt his feelings one night. "I love you," I said, anxious to let him know how sorry I felt for wounding him. "I receive that," he replied, looking at me steadily.

Ladies, the heart of a man is a mysterious thing. Men can seem so strong but crumble or lash out when they feel cornered or disrespected or hurt. Commitment scares them because they know no woman is perfect. They are not perfect. Sooner or later, disappointment will come—for all of us. Maybe that is why he never acknowledged me as a part of his life. I waited three years for a breakthrough.

> Patience can persuade a prince, and soft speech can break bones. (Proverbs 25:15 NLT)

I was determined to live out this verse.

It was not to be.

I did what God had specifically told me not to do . . . I showed the gentleman my anger because he decided I needed to step down from the worship band for the Saturday Bible study. That hurt me, and I made sure that he knew it. I still hoped we would be together. I had started repeatedly seeing a verse from the Bible—the one in Genesis that talks about the two becoming one flesh (Genesis 2:24). I also made the mistake of sharing how I felt about him to an older person I trusted to keep my confidence, but that person shared my words with him.

"I don't think you should come to the Bible study anymore," the gentleman said. Shocked, I slammed the phone down halfway through his phone message. I had gotten my breakthrough—just not the one I wanted. It got worse. One of the pastors called me in to meet with him. He said I could not be involved in any ministries for several weeks.

He had talked with the gentleman and his lady friend. They said it was best. As soon as I got the phone message, I knew things had changed between us. I did not want to force my presence on anybody who did not want me. There was no need for this. People would be told I could not be involved in any ministries. They would wonder why.

But the choice was not up to me. Again I felt the shame and embarrassment of being found wanting. Even now, the tears fall. I have never been the same since. The scars on my body have caused me great pain. Losing loved ones has shaken me. This chapter in my story has been the hardest to live and the hardest to write. I am glad this chapter of this book is almost over.

The two did "become one flesh." I saw them a year ago around Christmastime. Someone who knew them well told me they would be coming to a special gathering in a few days. After we talked, I walked away and headed for my car in the church parking lot.

*You need to go to this gathering,* God said to me.

Inwardly, I felt my body sink. I did not want to go. I had seen them a few times since their marriage and had spoken to them—well, mostly to him—in passing. I did not seek them out. I made a point not to do anything that would upset anyone. I could have lived the rest of my life without seeing them again. But those of us who know God know He always makes us do the hard stuff—the stuff we would rather not do.

When I saw the rainbow, I knew God was up to something.

Most winter days where I live in Southern California are sunny and mild, with a hint of warmth. This one had been cool and rainy. I had just left a mall—my least favorite place—to pick up a dress I could not get anywhere else. Now I had to navigate traffic and slippery roads to get to this gathering God had told me he wanted me to attend.

I looked at the address and set the GPS on my phone. I turned onto the already crowded boulevard and sighed. Then I saw it up ahead, slightly to my right. The multi-colored rainbow streamed from the clouds above it. I smiled. Rainbows always made me smile. They remind me that God is a promise maker. The closer I got to the house, the bigger the rainbow got . . . like it was leading me there.

When I went inside, I found out it was a Christmas party where they would have dinner, give gifts, have worship, and participate in a Bible study. It was like the old days, but I wanted to leave and just escape into the night. But I stayed. The gentleman and his wife had not arrived yet. I had to at least meet them and pay my respects.

When I saw them, I fought the urge to bolt. I smiled and said, "Hi." Both took a step back when they saw me. The lady quickly moved on with a smile to greet others in the room. He gave a little smile and said, "Hey," before ambling into the room. I continued to sit quietly in my chair, occasionally smiling and talking to people I knew.

After the chatting and dinnertime ended, we were all ushered into a back room for worship and a message. They also had a little ceremony where people could honor and share about people close to them who had died. It was painful and touching and a very needed time of memorial. Frankly, I did not know I needed the memorial until I was there. There is a grief that screams. But there is a grief that is silent and powerful, and it does not necessarily have to do with the death of a person.

The evening ended with prayer and Christmas presents. I think I offended the host, but I could not take a gift. I wanted no memento of the night. I had obeyed God's call to attend the gathering. I made my farewells quickly and walked purposely back to my car.

It was time to move on.

After seven years, my role as a classroom teacher and chapel leader changed to one of occasional instructor, substitute, and chaplain. The place and people that had seemed so hard to navigate had become like family to me, with relationships I cherish to this day. It amazes me still how life's beauty is often found in a valley—a place where you never thought you would be and never wanted to be.

But I was needed in the valley.

Dad was getting older. He was sassy and opinionated. He wanted to be as independent and as in control as possible. We all do, no matter what our age. But when your body does not cooperate and when your mind does not submit to physical weakness and limitation, that is not good for you or those around you.

Lanthe's health had declined too. She was able to experience three years of grace from dialysis, thanks to a kidney transplant. But she still suffered from lupus and its pain and symptoms. One spring she caught pneumonia. She was hospitalized for several days but finally recovered enough to go home.

Yet she was never the same. She developed severe back pain that took away much of her mobility and independence. She was in and out of hospitals. She even spent several weeks in a convalescent home—a devastating event for a woman forty-one years old. Just when it seemed like she had improved and would be released from the home, Lanthe was rushed to another hospital. The doctors discovered a deep infection in her back. They wanted to operate. She said no. I thought about my mom and how she had said no to a heart operation years ago. Near the end, she kept saying, "I'm tired." Looking at my sister, I finally understood.

Dad was Dad. Sassy and opinionated—and faithful. No matter what hospital or center or home my sister went to, Dad was there by her bedside—reading the Bible, watching television, or just sitting quietly—just like he did for his mom, his wife, and countless other relatives and friends throughout his life. Dad wore me out. I was not as faithful as he was.

Sleeping in hospital chairs is not comfortable. But I saw how important being uncomfortable can be. One night my sister was not doing too well emotionally. The nurse wanted my dad and me to stay the night with her. It was a long night. But as we sat with my sister, she said something that stuck with me. "I know you guys love me."

The presence of my dad and me was enough to prove to her that we loved her. In the months prior to her decline, she had committed her life to Christ. She even attended church with me. We went out to eat and shared things. That had rarely been a part of our relationship. I am thankful that we had those moments. I am eternally grateful that she asked God into her life when she did. I am glad she knew she was loved.

That made it easier to step away and leave her and Dad for a few weeks. I had finally scheduled a trip to Israel for November of that year. With my sister's hospital stays, I was unsure what to do. It did not seem right to be away from my sister and Dad, but I felt God saying I should go . . . that I needed to go. So when I landed in Tel Aviv one early evening, I wondered what God had in store for me. Trial and error had showed me that God is intentional. He always has a reason for what He does and for what He allows. I still believed He would call me to minister in Israel someday. Maybe the trip was preparation for that call.

It was not my first trip to Israel. I had visited twelve years before. I enjoyed the beautiful scenery and the historical places that I toured. But I experienced some prejudice from a few people during my time there. Their bias disappointed and shocked me. "You are very fat. What are you?" asked a woman seated near me in the hotel dining area. *What am I?* I'd never been asked that before. Outraged but dumbfounded, I ignored her question. I tried to ignore her too, though her comment stung.

Now I had returned and wondered if I would confront the same cutting words or even worse. After disembarking the plane and going through customs, I settled down in an area to wait for the people who would pick me up. I had booked the trip through a Christian tour company that specialized in organizing tours to the Holy Land. I would be meeting the in-country staff and a roommate I had yet to speak to.

Soon the guides, staff, and other tourists with my group arrived. They were friendly and reassuring. They promised they would take us to our hotel as soon as all the group members arrived. A younger gentleman and I struck up a conversation. He had left his home in England to travel and see biblical sites in Greece and Jordan. He was also a good soccer player and used his skills and love for the game to connect with young people. It was his unique way of sharing himself and God's love with others. I loved that.

He mentioned how the staff wanted people to lead morning devotions while we were traveling to our daily activities. I offered to do worship for the devotions. In a few minutes, he created a plan and shared it with the leaders. I smiled. While back home and packing for the trip, I noticed some worship song sheets in my closet. *Take them*, God's soft voice instructed me. I continued to look at the sheets. Hmm. Why would I do that? This is a trip. I paused and listened quietly. Then I picked up the folder filled with the sheets and stuffed them in my carry-on.

I felt happy that I had heard and obeyed God.

Our group was a mixture. There were Christians and Jews, Americans and Canadians, Black, White, and Asian, young and old. Though we were different, we were unified. Somehow there was always a song that someone said touched them or reflected a facet of their life. It awed me how God knew what a person needed to hear. Those morning devotions became my favorite part of the trip. I enjoyed meeting the Israelis we encountered. There was no prejudice or hurtful words. A young soldier even let me pray for her while my group was visiting the city of David one day. I appreciated my roommate too. She was a lovely young woman who served as a youth leader in her church and worked for a foreign consulate in central California. We shared many long evening talks in our hotel room.

Things got tougher when my health changed. Congestion and pain slowly enveloped my body. A trip to a park in the rain did not help. I worried that an infection in my keloids might flare up, causing more discomfort and embarrassment around my roommate. I had also called my dad. He seemed fine, and my sister's condition had not worsened. Nonetheless, my spirit felt disquieted, but I looked forward to returning one day to serve the Israeli people and to be baptized in the Jordan River.

Soon I left Israel, thankful for the people and places I had experienced there. God was right—as He always is. I needed that time away from hospitals and talking to doctors and running errands and doing things for my family. I slipped back into the routine of visiting my sister, either alone or with my dad. Although she was stable while I was away, she seemed less active and quieter than I recalled before the trip. A few days later, her kidneys stopped working.

"She's going down a little," one of the nurses said to me one night after I visited. I looked at her and considered what the nurse was really saying to me. My sister was dying. I knew that. God Himself had warned me death was near. A few days before the visit, I read in my Bible:

After this I looked, and there before me was a door standing open in heaven. (Revelation 4:1)

You leave a door open when you expect someone.

Then there was the teary-eyed young woman I saw outside the small hospital where my sister was a patient. I was headed to the front door and saw her semi-crouched against the outside wall with a phone in her hand. I did not know if I would be intruding or if I would be received. And, frankly, I had a lot on my mind. But I knew I could not leave the young woman alone. I cautiously walked up to her.

"What's the matter?" I asked gently.

"My dad just died," she said.

*Oh dear.* "Oh, I'm so sorry."

I stood talking with her. Her relatives would be coming a few minutes later. She gave me a brave little smile and then thanked me for stopping to speak with her. I tried to encourage her briefly one more time before walking inside to visit my sister. The thought came to me that soon my family would be the ones being comforted.

A week later I walked into the little ICU cubicle that served as my sister's room and recoiled. I almost did not recognize her. She had so many tubes, and she was swollen. Her doctor came and told me that fluid had built up in her body. Her body no longer could receive dialysis. The doctor and nurses asked about taking her off life support. I left and made the fifteen-minute drive home and spoke with my dad. I told him the situation. "She looks like a monster," I told him sadly, not knowing what else to say. "Okay," he replied and signed the papers. As I turned to leave, I glanced at him sitting on the edge of his bed. "I think my blood pressure is up," he said. I hesitated, hating to leave him. He told me to go back to the hospital. I drove back to the hospital and dropped off the papers and then headed back home to be with my dad.

I was in my room when the nurse called me. "She passed away three minutes ago."

"She did," I replied simply.

The nurse said I had to come back to the hospital to sign papers and to release her body to the funeral home. I sighed, told her I'd be on my way, and hung up.

Stopping at the door of my dad's room, I announced, "Daddy, Lanthe just died."

He flinched. A frown started at the corners of his mouth and spread. We discussed what mortuary to call, and I arranged for someone to meet me at the hospital.

When I got there, the receptionist who usually greeted me when I signed in left her seat and came to give me a hug. She had heard the code blue when my sister passed.

"I'm sorry," she said, almost crying herself.

I thanked her for her kindness. I would miss her. We talked many times when I came to visit my sister. I learned that she attended my church. She had been going through some hard things. I hoped she would be okay. When I entered the ICU, a nurse was preparing my sister for the mortuary. I kept my distance as I signed the papers.

"You are strong," one of the nurses said to me.

If she only knew.

"God makes me strong," I replied pointing upward. She nodded, then let me go on my way.

Driving back home through the mist and the rain, I tried to anticipate all that needed to be done. The arrangements. Meeting with the funeral director. Seeing the final resting place. And the phone calls. I would have to call my cousin and tell her Lanthe died. They were so close—far closer than my sister and I ever were.

When Lanthe was strong, she spent her time visiting my cousin and my cousin's children and grandchildren. Though single and never married, Lanthe embraced them as a beloved auntie who attended their events, traveled with them, bought them gifts, and shared in their joys and sorrows. Lanthe left them a legacy of love.

That is the message my cousin shared about my sister when we gathered to memorialize Lanthe inside the little Compton chapel a few days before Christmas. It was a small group of mostly extended family, former neighbors, and friends from work and church. I was thankful for all of them and grateful for the kindness and comfort they gave to my dad and me.

I ached for my dad and his pain.

In the span of a year, he had to bury his mother and his wife. Now, ten years later, he stood at the graveside of his youngest daughter. It is a place no parent wants to be. And no matter how much you love God and know that He loves you, it hurts. It just hurts. I can still see my dad slowly shaking his head in disbelief as we left Rose Hills Memorial Park and descended back into the valley below.

"If God wasn't God, I wouldn't fool with Him," one of my church friends said to me one day.

I smiled ruefully and laughed at her comment. I could relate. Yep, she spoke some truth right there. Can I shock you? Can I mess with your religion a little bit? Can I just be honest and tell you something?

God will disappoint you.

Sometimes it seems like He goes out of His way to rock your world. One minute you have a nice little suburban life where your needs are met and you can plan for your future. You go to church. You read your Bible. You spend time with God. You serve others. You do all the things everyone, including you, believes you should do. You even do what God says you should do.

Then your world turns.

You lose your job or you need to quit. The illness comes or becomes chronic. Accidents happen. You and your spouse grow apart, or you find it difficult to relate to your adult children with their different beliefs and ways of doing things. Maybe you have conflicts with people in church. Maybe you have turned thirty. Or forty. Or fifty. And you wonder what you will have to show for all those years of life.

Maybe God called you to leave your career or ministry. Maybe, like me, God didn't heal your keloids or your ailment or provide you a husband. Sometimes following God is hard. You expect so much of Him. I mean, He is God and the One who made the heavens and earth. He can do anything.

And He places you in a valley, and it feels like He is punishing you. It feels like He is abandoning you. It feels like He does not love you. Yet I am reminded that Jesus warned us—warned me—that we would be disappointed and that God would not always do what we want Him to do.

And blessed is the one who is not offended by me. (Matthew 11:6 ESV)

God will bless everyone who doesn't reject me because of what I do. (Matthew 11:6 CEV)

*God, I was offended. Forgive me.*

I wonder if anything could have kept me out of the valley. I wonder if there is something I could have done or should have done. Regret lays heavy on my soul. Perhaps those of you who have spent time in the low places can understand.

This I do know—God placed me in the valley. And it was no mistake. He had to. I had gotten too comfortable and too set in my ways. I wanted to be safe. I did not want to take risks. I did not want to live by faith. I should have known better.

But my righteous one will live by faith. (Hebrews 10:38)

As God's children, we need to trust and depend on Him. He desperately wants us to seek Him in everything and for everything. Because when we look to other things—like a job or a husband or even ministry—we easily lose our identity to the material and the temporary. We lean on our own limited understanding instead of God's infinite wisdom.

But God will always remind us that He is in control.

For me, God forced me to let go of the familiar. I had no choice but to deny myself and follow Him (Matthew 16:24). My middle-class existence gave me a false sense of security. I was never in control of anything. God gives us all the good stuff in our lives anyway. And if He gives them, He can take them away for His own good purposes.

God will always give us what we need.

I needed to be humbled. Expecting I would live a certain life was prideful. It was a boasting in a tomorrow that was never promised to me. So God did the opposite of what I expected or even wanted. Instead of sending me to Israel, He sent me to Harbor City. Instead of having me work with adults, God had me serve children. Instead of having a big ministry in another country, I ministered to my dad and sister. Instead of providing a husband, God kept me single.

He also kept me in the valley. A valley is a low area midway between mountains, hills, and waterways. Obstacles are there. Danger is there. A valley can be hard to navigate. Those who live there often find themselves hemmed in. And the only way out of a valley is through the valley.

Yet the God who places you in the valley will walk with you through its shadows.

You will have no doubt that He is there. His voice becomes clearer. His words become more precious. His presence glows even brighter. I saw Him. I saw Him in the children I taught, in the elders I comforted, and in my sister's new faith. I heard Him in church sermons and in worship songs and in people I met in stores.

God sustains you in the valley. He sends people and other means to care for your needs. He shows His faithfulness through human kindness and unexpected blessings. He comforts you when worries and grief consume you. He gives you the right Scripture just when you need to see and hear it. God gives you hope to persevere.

God reminded me that there was beauty in living life—even life in the valley. There was the beauty of new relationships and time with family and being used by Him to comfort others who may be in their own valleys. Even when the pain of our wounds and scars threaten to overwhelm us, we can know that nothing we go through is wasted. Our God is with us in the valley that is life. He is with us in the tension of what is and what is to come. There is much He wants to teach us and much He wants to do in, with, and through us.

Are you weary? I am weary.

But God is with me. He is with you. Giving up is no longer a choice. We have come too far to stop now. Besides, God will not forget us.

He promises to bring us out of the valley.

### "Do You See Me?"
By Denise Ann Goosby

"Be still and know," I hear You say,
But emptiness fills my heart.
I long for touch, a sweet embrace.
A kiss upon my brow.

I know You love me. Lord,
You gave Your life for me.
But does Your love mean
No one else can love me?

I don't know what to do.
The longing hurts so bad.
To think You won't come through,
Your promise not fulfilled.

That two become one,
Walking hand in hand,
Giving glory to God,
Sacred love in which to stand.

Is it too much to ask?
To be accepted as I am?
To be wanted and beloved?
To be held by my man?

Do You see me, Lord?
Do my tears move your heart?
Is it wrong to know I'm loved by another?

Do You see me, Lord?
Nothing is impossible with you,
So why am I still alone?

Life goes by so fast,
Just a mist that fades away.
And the things of earth won't last,
Can't replace Your love and grace.

Yet my heart longs to know
Someone has chosen me,
To be by my side
Till death do us part . . .

Do You see me, Lord?
Do my tears move your heart?
Is it wrong to know I'm loved by another?

Do You see me, Lord?
Nothing is impossible with You,
So why am I still alone?

I don't want to seem ungrateful.
You are so good to me.
Savior, Healer, Protector,
Your love has rescued me.

But if I am to be honest,
Then honest I will be.
Have You yet to find him,
The one who can love me?

Is there one who can love me? . . .

No eye has seen, no one can dream
What God does for His people.
You are faithful, You keep Your word.
Please help my unbelief, Lord.

Let me remember all You've done.
Let me remember Who You are.
Let me remember my El Roi,
The God who sees me.
The One who has chosen me . . .

I know You see me, Lord.
My tears move Your heart.
It's not wrong to be loved by another.

I know You see me, Lord,
Nothing is impossible with You.
You promise I am never alone.

I'm Yours, and I'm never alone.

## Devotional

### What Can I Hear from a Bone?

*They say, "Our bones are dried up and our hope is gone; we are cutoff... I will put my Spirit in you, and you will live, and I will settle you in your own land. Then you will know that I the LORD have spoken, and I have done it, declares the LORD."*
Ezekiel 37:11, 14

If you wait long enough . . . if I you push far enough . . . if you dig deep enough . . . God will show you something.

We enter life's valleys, and all we see are the bones scattered all around us. We see broken bodies and dead dreams. We see our finances drained and our resources depleted. We see dashed hopes and unfulfilled promises. We see ourselves seemingly abandoned and left to fend for ourselves.

That is when our God shows up.

When we least expect it.

When our hope is as dry as a bone.

The God who placed us in the valley knows our end from the beginning. He has already arranged a way of provision and escape from our circumstances. He longs to show Himself as our champion and defender. But God is a great Father and a master teacher. He intentionally sets us in our valleys so we can learn lessons that will prepare us for the future blessings He has planned for us. He teaches us to trust Him, to walk humbly by His side, and to look to Him as our ultimate source—as our life.

Merriam-Webster Dictionary says a bone is more than a part of our skeleton. It is part of our "core" and our "essence." It is "the most deeply ingrained part."

It is where we know that something is real. In the valley, we know that God is real. He does for us what nobody else can. He sustains. He does miracles. He sends the right people at the right time. He comforts us when we are utterly comfortless.

God takes the tired, dry, scattered bones of our lives and rebuilds them into something we could have never imagined possible. We just need to hold on. We need to see with our faith. Once again, those dry bones will live. We will live. You will live.

God will resurrect you and give you a reason to move on and move forward.

## Questions to Ponder in Your Heart

What have you learned from your valley?

How did God make Himself real to you in your valley?

How is God leading you through and out of your valley?

## Prayer

*Father God, I confess that sometimes I am disappointed in You, especially here in this valley.* I wonder what I have done. I long for deliverance. Help me, Father, to be still. Help me to learn what You know I need to learn as I journey through the valley. Show me how faithful and merciful You can be. Revive these bones of mine and give me hope. Amen.

## Memory Verse

> Even though I walk through the valley of the shadow of death, I will fear no evil, for you are with me; your rod and your staff, they comfort me. You prepare a table before me in the presence of my enemies; you anoint my head with oil; my cup overflows. Surely goodness and mercy shall follow me all the days of my life, and I shall dwell in the house of the LORD forever. (Psalm 23:4–6 ESV)

# Chapter 7

# IS THIS THE END OR THE BEGINNING?

*For everything there is a season, and a time for every matter under heaven.*
Ecclesiastes 3:1 ESV

"*I can't get rid of* my water, baby," my dad groaned to me one morning.

I looked at him questionably, not understanding what he was telling me. I started to ask him what he meant. Then it struck me: he couldn't empty his bladder. Fear entered the pit of my stomach as I edged closer to my dad.

"You need to go to the emergency room," I said sternly, trying to head off my dad's protests.

"Maybe I can wait a little longer and see what happens," he replied, trying to smile but clearly in pain. "Come on, Dad, let's go." Thankfully, he no longer fought me. I helped him get dressed and got him into the car.

I had reached that point in life where I was parenting my dad.

Neither one of us was happy. I went months—sometimes years—without working. When I did, it was part-time with little pay. Dad wanted to leave my place to go and fix up the house he raised me in and live in it by himself. He spent all his savings to do it. Dad almost lost the home until God led me to speak with a lady at church to help him keep it.

Unfortunately, his house that he had paid off years ago now had a mortgage on it. That meant we needed tenants to live in it and help us pay bills. I had to collect money from them. Sometimes these renters did not pay on time or purposely chose not to pay the amount that was due. Dad and I lived on his social security and pension and whatever we got in rent.

It scared me when my dad would drive. I tried to go with him as much as possible, which bugged him royally. If I happened to be working or running errands, he would go off on his own. One night he went to a local store. Someone ran into him and tried to blame him for the accident. A kind woman witnessed the whole incident. She said she would call her motorcycle buddies to come and make sure my dad was safe and not taken advantage of. God's deliverance comes in many ways.

A couple of times Dad got mad and just took off walking down the street. It amazed me that the same man I struggled to pick up when he fell or could not get himself out of the bathtub could move with such speed . . . and disappear so quickly. But he did. He had a cousin who lived about four or five blocks away. I worried he would try to visit him. He sometimes ended up a few houses down at one of my neighbors. Just like a parent, I was so angry when he ran off and so thankful when he returned safe and unharmed.

Fighting me was Dad's way of keeping control. I knew that in my head. I also suspected Dad's thinking was impaired. A doctor later told me Dad had early stages of dementia. Yet my heart felt wounded. I loved my dad. I wanted to help him. He did not see it that way. He said he was disappointed in me. That I was "living off of him" and taking advantage of him. The dad who had protected me as a child now saw me as his biggest threat.

But now his bladder did not work, and I had to get him to a hospital.

When we got to the hospital, they worked on him right away. There had been little time to spare. His bladder could have easily burst. I thought they would give him medicine to help him, but they were forced to put in a catheter—a painful procedure that neither of us was prepared for. I felt so sorry for my dad. I wanted to take his pain away. All I could do was try to keep his spirits up and to encourage him to hold on until things were better and the catheter could be removed.

The emergency room doctor recommended Dad be examined by a specialist who opted to do a same-day surgery to find out what was causing the blockage. I remember driving through the early morning darkness to the center where Dad would have his operation. I remember seeing Dad lying in bed with a bluish cap on his head as he was prepped for surgery. And I remember the numbness I felt when the specialist told me that the blockage was cancerous.

My dad had cancer.

The weight of the moment rendered me speechless. I did not want to think too far ahead. I did not want to think about what my dad would experience nor how it would be to watch him go through it. I knew I had to let the owners at the Christian school know right away. I had just started working there again part-time in the afternoon with their fourth-grade class. I would have to balance that with my dad's doctor visits and upcoming cancer surgery and follow-up care.

Dad had two surgeries. One was for a hernia that needed to be repaired before his bladder could be operated on. Then he had the cancer surgery, and he was in the hospital for several days following the operation. Dad was a fighter. I do not know too many people of any age—let alone a man of eighty-five—who could have survived. I am grateful for the doctor who operated on him. I knew Dad was in good hands. The doctor said he asked God how to best treat my dad. He was kind and compassionate toward us.

The doctor wanted to do one more surgery on my dad. He had gotten a lot of the cancer the first time. He felt that with this next surgery he could remove most of, if not all of, what was left. But Dad would not go back for another operation. He still had to use a catheter. The pain and lack of control and disappointment that his body would never be or do what it once did was bitter for him. I could see it in his face.

It did not seem fair.

My dad was the one who had taken care of family and friends and even complete strangers. He had given money, spent time with the sick, conducted funerals, attended events, prayed for others, and taught God's Word. He had been faithful. Even in his sickness and old age, he still loved God. He sang his hymns and spirituals, watched church on television, and read his Bible. He still had great expectations of God.

Dad began to tell me about a recurring dream.

God had showed him a blue bird that flew around a beautiful large ranch house. Dad said that house was for him. He wanted to find it. A couple of times, he asked me to drive him to where he thought that house was located. We drove eastward into the suburbs of southeast Los Angeles County that were once rancheros and dairy farms when California had just become a state. Dad searched the scenery as we drove by. But the beautiful home Dad looked for so earnestly—the one that God said was his—would not be found on earth.

God had been showing me things too.

He showed me through Dad's declining health and needed care that I needed to sell my home. Dad did not want to sell his own house, which caused contention at times in our relationship. Moving seemed the only solution. With the money, perhaps I could move us both into a senior apartment or assisted living community. My concern was that my house needed work done before it could be sold, and I did not have money to do that. But God worked through the son of the owner of the Christian school where I worked, who offered to front me the money and do the remodeling and work on the house. When it sold, I would pay him back. He also arranged for a realtor to show the house to prospective buyers and handle the sale for me. Everything was falling into place one step at a time.

My dad, however, was not pleased. He did not like the idea of moving away. He had his heart set on going back to his own house.

I also think he wanted to avoid living anyplace associated with the words *senior* or *assisted*. He tried to bring in another realtor to sell the house—someone who had helped us tremendously in the past. At eighty-eight, he was still fighting for control. But the day came when he had no choice but to relinquish that control.

I had just said goodbye to the would-be realtor and plopped down on my couch. Suddenly, I heard a sound behind me and turned around. My dad was semiconscious and slumped off the dining room chair. I moved to try and keep him from falling, but I did not have the strength.

"Dad!" I yelled, frightened he had hurt himself.

"Dad! Dad!" My fear intensified.

I couldn't help but wonder. *Would this be the day I lost my dad? Would he die right in front of me?*

I dialed 9-1-1. I had made such a call a couple of times before when my dad had fallen or had some issue with his heart or blood pressure. The paramedics would come and check him out, and he would refuse to go to the hospital. This time was different. They came and examined him and immediately took him to the nearest hospital that would receive him. I thought about what belongings and documents Dad and I would need and gathered them up. Then I headed to the hospital.

When I got to the emergency room, I found the little cubicle where my dad was being treated. One of the paramedics who transported him told me he'd woken up in the ambulance and had a fit. He did not know where he was, where he was going, and why he was in an ambulance. *Oh boy, here it comes.* I sighed inwardly. When I saw Dad and asked him how he felt, he scolded me.

"Why did you put me through this?" he asked, his voice shaky with age and anger. All I could do is look at him.

My dad rarely scolded me when I was a child.

I can only remember him spanking me once or maybe twice. They were brief bursts of anger when I had been disrespectful to him. Even then, I felt no fear, unlike with my mom. Somehow I knew my dad would never hurt me, abuse me, or make me feel unloved.

There were two times when I felt afraid with my dad as a child. The first is when he and Mom had argued and Dad moved out of the house. He stayed in a mobile home park for a couple of days. I guess he needed time to calm down and collect his thoughts. I remember him coming by the house to get me and take me to the park. We spoke, though what we said escapes me. I can still recall crying as he talked. I wanted my dad home with me. A few days later, he returned. He never again mentioned that time away from the family.

The second time was when I came home from school one day and found out that Dad had shot someone. Several weeks before, one of the neighbors behind us started brandishing and firing a gun. My aunt's family next door often saw the neighbor and would flee into the house. One day while I was visiting, the neighbor pulled out the gun, so we took cover and then ran into the house. Well, they ran into the house. I froze. I just remember doors slamming and seeing my uncle Willie open the back door and move as quickly as his elderly body allowed. Apparently, something similar had taken place while I was at school. Dad had enough and decided to act. He was arrested.

When I got home, family members were discussing how to bail Dad out. Worried about my dad and wondering if I would ever see him again, I cried and looked at the relatives gathered in my aunt's house. A few hours later, Dad walked silently into my aunt's kitchen and stood with his arms folded behind him, leaning against a wall. He stared straight ahead. Adults were talking around me, but I could not take my eyes off my dad.

After a few minutes, the talking stopped. My dad moved away from the wall. Someone said "thank you," and my family left to make the short walk back home. The legal situation with the neighbor eventually resolved itself. I do not know how. I just know that when the day came for my dad to go to court, he dressed up in a gray suit and said he would trust God.

He returned home from the hearing and went on with his life. I heard him talking about the situation with the husband of his cousin, who was a fellow minister. I think he wanted my dad to share how God had brought him through the experience. "I need a little more time," my dad replied, leaning back into the lawn chair. I never knew if Dad testified about the incident, but he did go back to preaching and ministering to others. He eventually helped his cousin's husband at his church. Dad served as president of the prayer ministry and helped with Wednesday afternoon food distribution to the needy.

That was the dad I knew and loved.

Now Dad was scared and confused and, I later learned, had suffered a cardiac episode. Whether he accepted it or not, he needed care. My dad stayed in the hospital several days. I thought he would return home. Until the house was sold, I would need to care for him. But one morning I read a verse in the Bible. It was as if God was speaking to me: "It is not good for the man to be alone" (Genesis 2:18).

I could no longer take care of my dad alone. I had neither the strength nor the medical expertise to give him what he needed. His doctors said he would need rehabilitation. I was told to look for a center for my dad. It would be paid for under his health coverage. But when Dad's transport came to take him to the center, I felt like I had failed him. My feelings intensified when I saw him in his room at the center. It was tiny and his bed was broken. My heart broke. Because it was close to midnight, my dad would not have a proper bed until morning.

I wanted him out of there. I sat by his bed all night watching him and watching the clock. I wanted to find him someplace else to stay. When morning came, I made it clear to the staff on duty that I wanted my dad to have a new bed and to be moved to another facility. I made some calls, but no other centers were available. Dad's nurses urged me to keep him there. I hesitated but decided to take things day by day.

It was near the Christian school where I worked and about a thirty-five-minute drive to my house—which would not be my house much longer. At one point, the house's interior needed to be painted.

I had to move into a motel for a week. I found one a mile or two up the road from my dad. I settled into a routine of doing morning errands and appointments. In the afternoon, I visited Dad. Sometimes I would sit with him while he ate lunch or did activities in the community room. A few times, I wheeled him outside to the patio, and we sat in the sunshine, but mostly I just sat by his bed watching his roommate's television and attending to his needs.

My hope was to move my dad to a nicer place. My dad had cared for me and our family as only an imperfect yet good father could . . . with all his heart. I wanted the best for this dad, this man whom I loved despite the heartaches and hardships I experienced in trying to care for him.

It was not to be.

Dad was getting weaker. He no longer wanted to get out of bed. He no longer could get out of bed. He still remembered the little blue bird and the ranch house. He asked me to try and find it. I just smiled and looked at him. One day as I was walking to my dad's room, I stopped his nurse and asked how he was doing. Half looking at me, with a gentle smile on her face, she replied, "I think he's getting ready to go home."

I saw it too. I had asked the visiting pastor to stop by and see my dad a couple of times. My dad loved talking about the Bible. He enjoyed speaking with ministers and people who loved God. This pastor had been particularly kind and concerned for my dad. I knew the pastor's mom was in the hospital. I admired how he could care for others when his own heart was hurting. The pastor ministering to my dad helped me begin to release him into the hands of God. That is where Dad wanted to be—where he belonged.

It was a clear, crisp blue-sky morning that greeted me as I took my suitcase and placed it in my dad's silver Ford Taurus. I had spent the night in Los Alamitos after attending a Christmas concert at a nearby church the night before. My dad—Papa—had looked ill the night before. I wanted to stay with him. But I sensed God pushing me away. I needed a respite, an evening devoid of the sights and sounds of the facility where Dad had spent the last three months.

Now I felt God urging me to get to my dad.

In His still small voice, God whispered that I needed to get back to the center around 9:00 a.m. I drove determinedly westward through the traffic. Soon I saw the Palos Verdes peninsula rising in the distance. At its foot was the center where Papa was. I smiled slightly when I saw the open parking space near my dad's room. That did not happen often.

Papa looked tired.

As I entered his room, I noticed that his head rested crookedly on a pillow. A touch of melancholy hit me. Daddy LC was my champion and defender. When I was not sure God loved me, I knew my daddy did. My mom had suffered several miscarriages. I was the first baby who survived pregnancy. I was born a week before Christmas, and my first present was a Christmas tree from my daddy.

"Is he born?"

That's what my mom said my dad asked the doctor when he announced my birth. I loved the mirth in my mom's voice as she told me. No, I was not my father's son. But I was his oldest daughter—and the son he never had. I liked playing with my dolls and toys, but nothing compared to going fishing with my dad at the beach or at a lake. I loved those warm, sunny days of laughter and excitement spent by his side, especially when I got a fish.

Dad's presence filled my days. Even now I picture him watering the front lawn. I see him teasing my mom. I see him preaching God's Word in church or praying to Father God with tears streaming down his weathered, brown face. I see him at my high school graduation watching me give the valedictorian speech and walking up the hill to see me receive my college diploma. I also see him, head bowed, at my mom's grave and at the grave of my sister.

I knew I was seeing him for the last time this side of heaven.

I sat beside him on the bed. His roommate's TV showed pictures of the latest brush fire. It was three weeks before Christmas but sunny and hot. The sound of feet walking on linoleum got my attention as a resident and a nursing assistant shuffled by.

Dad's breathing became more and more rough . . . labored. He seemed to be fighting for every breath he could take. I held his hand, glancing at the news, glancing at him. I told him how much I loved him. I thanked him for being a good daddy. I thanked God for giving him to me. Soon Dad's breathing stopped, and he was still.

"Daddy?" I said gently, shaking him softly.

I waited a few moments. I saw a nurse's assistant in a room across the way and went to her. She saw my face and was moving before I told her my dad was not breathing. The next few minutes were filled with nurses scurrying around and checking on Dad.

Someone decided to call it. He had died. His body remained, but he had left it and was now present with the Lord. Nurses and attendants offered their condolences. I made a few phone calls. One of the male attendants asked if he could say goodbye to my dad. I thought that was nice, and it felt like a tribute to my dad.

I stayed with my dad until the mortuary people came to take him. I did not want him to be alone. I had begun arrangements for his service and final resting place the week before. The site was a beautiful, lush memorial park with grassy hills and the waters of the Los Angeles Harbor in the distance. It was not the ranch house with the blue bird Dad had envisioned, but I suspected he saw that being with Jesus in heaven was far better.

I watched as the mortuary driver loaded Dad into the white van that would carry him a few miles away. As the van turned to leave, I saluted my dad—my papa. My dad proudly served in the army during the Korean War. He would tell me stories about living on a ship. He told me of how someone stole his mosquito net and how he was forced to protect himself under a hot, woolen blanket. He described walking the Golden Gate Bridge back to his barracks. I wanted to honor his service. I wanted to honor him. Death had parted us. But I knew my father's God was also my God—the God who conquered death and promises to make all things new. There was no need to say goodbye.

"See you soon, Dad. See you soon."

God sends people for your life.

Though God loves us supremely, He knows it is not good for us to be alone. He puts people in our path who will love and care for us—people who will encourage us, advocate for us, and walk beside us through life's valleys. For much of my life, my dad did that for me. And in those final years, I did that for him. I think God uses our wounds and scars to prepare us to serve others, especially those who suffer.

God had placed me in the valley not only for me but for my dad.

When I did not have money or a position or even knowledge, I could still give my daddy my presence. I could listen to his stories, spend time with him, and bear witness to God's goodness through Dad's testimonies and songs. Nothing more. There is infinite value in just being a human being and for being exactly who you are.

Do you know you are precious just because you are you?

We forget that. We often feel we must do something, be something, or have something to offer to be worthy of someone's time and attention. But that's not how God sees us—not the Father. Before Adam and Eve did anything, God pronounced them good. Before we entered the wombs of our mothers, God knew us and believed in us and chose us to tell others about Him—despite our scars and our flaws.

Those who love God speak often of Him. I enjoyed that about my dad. He did not outgrow His need for God. Even in his pain and fear and struggle for control, he looked to God. He talked to Him and depended on Him for everything. He read and studied the Bible. And when he was no longer able to turn its pages, he still carried the words in his heart. Old age and dementia are no match for God's grace and love.

Let us hold on to that as we walk through our winter years. Let us remember that even with our old age and gray hair and scars, God is with us. We just need to humble ourselves enough to receive the people and things God brings into our lives—even when they hurt us. God says our latter days can be greater than our former days. If we just hold on. If we just don't give up. If we trust Him.

Our lives can preach a powerful lesson to others. That alone makes our wounds and our scars worth it.

### "Daddy"
(Tag line from "Blessed Assurance")
By Denise Ann Goosby

You loved me before I even knew what love was,
Even before I knew God.
You were all to me.
You loved me before I knew what love was,
Even before I knew myself.
You were all to me.
Nearly three years now since you left, Daddy.
Images fill my mind
Of you smiling, of you crying, of the pain in your eyes.

Sometimes the ache comes softly . . . floating on the wind.
Sometimes it's a flood trying to draw me under again.
But it's only because I love you still.
You know, love never dies.
And even though I miss you still,
I know it's not goodbye.

Cause you left a legacy that money cannot buy.
Your hugs and kisses let me know I mattered to you.
Times we spent fishing or lifting praises to the sky,
Oh, Daddy, did you know Jesus shone from your eyes?

You were always there when I needed you,
In good times and in bad.
Watching me receive my diploma,
Standing by momma's graveside.

In the latter years as the losses mounted
You never lost your faith.
Loving God and loving others,
Your example I can never replace.

But what I can do is follow you
As you faithfully followed Christ.
Knowing my God is my father's God,
And I'll see you once again.

Cause you left a legacy that money cannot buy.
Your hugs and kisses let me know I mattered to you.
Times we spent fishing or lifting praises to the sky,
Oh, Daddy, did you know Jesus shone from your eyes?

It's hard carrying on without you.
Even now the tears are going to fall.
But the Father of us both holds me closely,
And He's my all and all . . .

Thank you for your legacy that money cannot buy.
Thank you for your hugs and kisses that mattered so much to me.
The times we spent fishing or lifting praises to the sky,
Oh, Daddy, thank you for Jesus—He shone from your eyes.

Tag line:
This is my story, this is my song,
Praising my Savior all the day long.
This is my story, this is my song,
Praising my Savior all the day long.

### Devotion

### Abba Father

*I will be a Father to you, and you will be my sons and daughters, says*
*the LORD Almighty.*
2 Corinthians 6:18

None of us grew up with perfect fathers.

My dad was a loving father and a wonderful provider, but he still hurt me. He still spoke words that pierced my soul. He forgot important dates. He looked at me with disappointment. He sinned and missed the mark. Some of you have experienced far worse than this. You have suffered abandonment, abuse, and alienation from the one who should love you most. You have been scarred by your father.

I wish to God you had never had to experience that.

I wish I could reach through these pages and wrap my arms around you and tell you how much you are loved and honored and valued. I wish I could heal your pain . . . just snatch it away. I do know someone who can do great things with pain . . . someone who can step into your hurt and scars and broken heart and bring a comfort and beauty that will take your breath away.

> So you have not received a spirit that makes you fearful slaves. Instead, you received God's Spirit when he adopted you as his own children. Now we call him, "Abba, Father." (Romans 8:15 NLT)

This Father will never leave you. This Father will never forget you. This Father will never seek your harm—only your good. This Father engraves you on the palm of His hand. This Father sees and catches your every tear, hears and answers your every prayer. This Father waits and mourns for you when you turn away . . . and runs back to you when you make the slightest turn in His direction. This Father watches over you, sings over you, and forgives you—every sin as far as the east is from the west.

He is Abba Father. Your Father. A perfect Father.

Open your heart and arms and receive the fullness of His love. Right here. Right now. Today.

## Questions to Ponder in Your Heart

How do you feel when you see or hear the word "father"?

How does your relationship with your earthly father influence your relationship with your Abba Father?

What is the one thing you long to hear from your earthly father? From your Abba Father?

## Prayer

*Dear Father, Abba, it is hard to believe that You love me—even my scars.* I have never been loved like this before. You love me just because I am me. I am not used to that. Frankly, it scares me. It makes me hesitate to receive Your love. Forgive me for those times I turn away from You. Help me to remember that You give good gifts to Your children. All I have to do is to ask you. Amen.

## Memory Verses

> The LORD will guide you always; he will satisfy your needs in a sun-scorched land and will strengthen your frame. You will be like a well-watered garden, like a spring whose waters never fail. (Isaiah 58:11)

> Therefore I am now going to allure her . . . and will make the Valley of Achor a door of hope. (Hosea 2:14, 15)

# Chapter 8

# AM I AT THE EDGE OF THE JORDAN?

*All my longings lie open before you, LORD; my sighing is not hidden from you.*
Psalm 38:9

*The driveway to the Motel* 6 came quick. I made a sharp right and headed to the now familiar space in the southwest corner of the lot. Slowly, almost painfully, I climbed out of the driver's seat. I shut and locked the door of my dad's Taurus and headed to my room. The noise of people and cars and life danced around me, but I felt numb. When my key buzzed green, I pushed open the door, closed it behind me, and gingerly sat in a chair.

How did I get here?

More importantly, where would I go from here? The house I had bought as a young teacher nineteen years ago was about to close escrow. In a few days, it would no longer be my home. Sentimentality aside, that was a good thing. Until the money from the sale came through, I could not move into the new apartment I had found. Motel 6 was home, at least for a few more days. Normally, that would not bother me. I had already been there a week. It was in a familiar area. I could

run errands, do business, and see my dad at the center and be back by early evening for dinner.

Dad.

Papa's eighty-eight years on earth culminated in a victorious eternity with Jesus. That made me smile. Yet sitting in that motel room after saying goodbye to my dad—the one person who I never doubted loved me—I couldn't help but think what my life would be like without him. Without my "Moses." My leader. My shepherd. I owed so much to this man who parented me and took care of me and introduced me to my Savior God. Without him I felt incomplete. Adrift. Uncertain.

God, however, knew exactly what I needed to do. He guided me before I even knew I needed direction. A month before Dad passed, I saw an apartment for rent on the internet. It looked safe, well kept, with parking and amenities. After I toured it, I sensed that I should apply for it. The young man who gave me the tour encouraged me to fill out an application and submit to a credit check. Silently, I did and worried that I would be embarrassed and disappointed when I was turned down. I was accepted. People, that should not have happened. But it did.

A week before Dad passed, I sensed I needed to go and speak with someone at the memorial park up the road from the center. I stopped in to just check on their pricing and services. I ended up making all the arrangements. I even picked a suit for my dad to wear. The people who helped me said I could pay when I got the money from my house sale.

Yes, God's timing was perfect. Papa died on a Wednesday. The money for my house came on Friday. By Tuesday I had paid for Dad's service, gotten new furniture for my apartment, and moved into my new place. I was overwhelmed and exhausted and thankful that I could be still and just breathe. For a week, I slept soundly—even with my keloids. I used the time to rest and to plan Dad's funeral.

When that day came, I drove the mile north to my church in Gardena and joined with friends, coworkers, former neighbors, and supporters for Dad's homegoing celebration. The musicians did a

beautiful job playing the songs. It was so healing for me to join them on vocals. I enjoyed watching the video of my dad's life. I did not feel sad but instead felt proud that he had lived and that his life had touched my life.

The hardest part of the day was at the gravesite as I watched them lower Dad's casket into the ground and cover it with dirt. My heart broke anew, my throat closed, and the tears squirted from my eyes. I did not expect that. I mean, my daddy was in heaven. But grief is grief. Three years later, I still miss him.

That's what happens when someone loves you well.

The next several months became a quiet blur. I still had Dad's affairs to put in order. There was his house and the renter I had to check on. I still did not know what I would do for the rest of my life . . . if I would go back to teaching or pursue missionary work.

Again God intervened.

God shepherded me through the grief and solitude. He brought people into my life and gave me new experiences to enjoy. A former neighbor invited me to a Bible study called Journey of Purpose. Every Tuesday night at 7:00 p.m. for seven weeks a group of us young and middle-aged women met in a church dining hall to eat, worship, and talk about how to use our gifts and talents for the kingdom of God. The ache of losing my dad and being alone was replaced with hope. God had not forgotten me. He had not forgotten my dreams to sing, travel, and help others.

"You know, ministries have come out of this study," a woman encouraged me before the teaching began that first night.

Several weeks later, I was reading my morning devotions. Into my mind came the thought to start a nonprofit called Healing Song Ministries. It would be a music therapy ministry that catered to seniors, veterans, and those who were hurting. God confirmed this call through His Word, circumstances, and others.

By the time the study ended, Healing Song Ministries had a logo, a legal filing, and a small support team. Our first event was a house concert in my apartment's community room. In the meantime

as I listened to Christian radio, I was continually hearing about a new nonprofit management degree that Biola University started the previous year.

Smiling to myself, I marveled at God's timing and His sense of humor. A few weeks later, I attended an informational meeting at Biola about the program. I had a month to fill out the application, get my transcripts, and request letters of recommendation. I scrambled to get the paperwork done.

"Yes!" I screamed as I read the acceptance letter. I could move forward now. God had provided. The sale of my house meant I had the money to go to school and fund the nonprofit. I could do this.

*I can't do this,* I wailed silently, erasing the equation on my paper. The tears started falling slowly at first but quickened as panic set in. I glanced at my classmates around me, roughly scraping a fresh stream of moisture from my face. I looked at the professor as she alternated between writing on the whiteboard and explaining the accounting problems on the worksheet.

I should have known.

Getting into college was not the hard part. Filling out applications and submitting essays and transcripts was tedious. I had done that thirty years ago. But that was before twenty years of teaching. That was before being a caregiver. That was before Dad died and before I had moved from my home. That was before everything I knew had been upended and before the calling had come.

*I'm a word person, not a business person. Why am I sitting here in an accounting class?* I sighed resignedly.

I already knew the answer: God.

Who else would make me go back to college at fifty-three? I should be planning my retirement. Now I was starting over with no parents, no husband, and no safety net. I still feel that way. But those who sow in tears will reap with songs of joy (Psalm 126:5).

My tears in accounting class were not wasted. With God's grace and the help of my teachers, I got through that class and the others that followed. As I moved deeper into my studies and calling, God worked deeper in me.

He reminded me that I did not have to prove myself to Him. I did not have to be perfect. I did not have to fear He would abandon or reject me if I failed. I always took pride in being a good student. My identity could no longer be in what I accomplished. It had to be in God and in being His child and a vessel of service (2 Corinthians 4:7). What mattered was what He could do through me. God sees the potential within us. Our competence is in Him (2 Corinthians 3:5).

*I have the perfect job for you.* God would often whisper to me during my morning time with Him. I smiled, comforted that God would lead me to a place where I could flourish.

In May 2020, I graduated with a master's degree in nonprofit management. I thought I knew what the next step in my life would be. I thought I would grow Healing Song Ministry or work for a bigger nonprofit or teach community college. That seemed like the reasonable, sensible thing for a middle-aged woman to do. You do what is safe. Does that make sense to you? It certainly made sense to me.

But God's way is often not our way. What is safe for us, God may consider foolhardy because it takes us out of His will.

Instead of moving me forward into the nonprofit world, God took me back to the future to my first love of writing. He stirred my heart to learn more. I devoured books on writing and publishing. I attended online writers conferences. I joined writing groups. I took classes and signed up with a writing coach. Someone set up a simple website, and then one of my professors introduced me to a woman whose company transformed my website into a beautiful and growing platform for my writing, publishing, and singing business ministry—Denise's Healing Journey. This book is part of the first fruits of that venture.

When I began following Christ as a younger woman, I looked forward to what God would do in my life. No longer would I have to

worry about my looks or my weight or my ethnicity or anything else holding me back because God can do anything. He can give me favor. He can open doors that no man can shut. He can send people for my life. He can get me married. He can heal.

I have finally lived long enough to see that God has given me a beautiful life.

He blessed me with a wonderful career as an educator of adults and children. He allowed me to see places that many people in my hometown of Compton, California, never see. Now that I'm in my fifties, He allowed me to get a new degree, start a nonprofit, and restart a writing career. God has also seen fit to let me outlive my parents and younger sister. I am still waiting for marriage. The healing for my keloids has yet to come.

But I will sing of God's goodness.

The water feels good. In the shower, my voice trails off. It's time to get out. But the irony of the moment is not lost on me. I sing about God's goodness while continuing to suffer, but I rejoice that I am still here. I can choose to see the goodness of the Lord in the life I live. Surely there is a message in that.

Later in the morning, I find myself reading a devotion by author Kay Warren, wife of Pastor Rick Warren of well-known Saddleback Church in Southern California. She talks about how dealing with her son's suicide and her earlier battle with breast cancer equipped her to comfort and encourage others. She was equipped because she chose to give God her pain and take the comfort God Himself had given her to help others.[5]

To God our scars are something to celebrate. Our scars are living metaphors of our lives, are they not? They tell the world that we are warriors and that we have fought battles. We are stronger than we

---

5  Kay Warren Daily Hope August 2020

look, and we may suffer long, but we also endure. We do not give up, because the God who lives through us won't let us.

Beloved ones, do not be ashamed of your scars. Do not be ashamed of your life. It is beautiful. You are beautiful. Your God—the perfection of beauty—says so. And He does not lie. You need to receive this. God is not ashamed of you (Hebrews 2:11).

> We are confident that God is able to orchestrate everything to work toward something good and beautiful when we love Him and accept His invitation to live according to His plan. (Romans 8:28 VOICE)

He has done that for me. He will do that for you.

My friends, thank you for joining me on this journey. Let us resolve to be the ones who wear our scars for Jesus. I want that for you. I want it for me. I want to be *that one*. The one who bravely, though with tears, bears the scars God has given me knowing that Jesus bravely bore His scars for me. I want to be the one who, for the joy set before me, endures my cross and inspires others to carry theirs. I want to be the one who points others to the goodness of God.

Therein lies the beauty.

## "Be Still"
By Denise Ann Goosby

Sometimes I am afraid to be still.
Even when I am not moving, my soul is restless.
My heart is troubled.
My mind races with what I did or should have done.
Regrets tumble inside my head like loose trash blowing in the wind.
Just a blowing . . .

But when I allow myself to be still,
I am struck by how powerful I feel.
I sense the peace lingering on the edge of my spirit,
Waiting for me to give it permission to assert itself.
My heart regains its normal rhythm.
My mind is settled.
All because I've chosen to be still . . .

To be still is to know.
To be still is to trust.
To be still is to believe.
To be still is to relinquish control—
To God.

To be still is to know I am safe.
That I am loved.
That I am forgiven.
That I won't be disappointed.
I won't be disappointed.

# Devotion

## Beauty in Life's Transitions

*Even to your old age and gray hairs I am he, I am he who will sustain you. I have made you and I will carry you; I will sustain you and I will rescue you.*
Isaiah 46:4

Seeing the beauty in the life you live means you will need to navigate life's transitions. Psalm 75:6–7 tells us that promotion—a transition from one place to another—comes from God. It is His work to use that transition—an affliction, a move, a new job, even death itself—as a bridge to get us to the place He has prepared us to be. God used my scars, including the death of my dad, to propel me into places I had never been and to people I had never met so I could do the things He had already planned for me to do (Ephesians 2:10).

God will do the same for you.

Beauty lies hidden in this transition. So does fear. You will feel afraid, but do not let that stop you. Have courage. Have hope. Know that God is with you. Know that He will send the people and resources you need to move forward. Prepare yourself, but stay open to the unexpected. Most importantly, put God first. Listen to Him by sitting still, praying, and reading the Bible. Then, when He says go, you go. Trembling, with tears or with supernatural boldness, move forward. Your time is now.

Don't waste a moment of it.

### Questions to Ponder in Your Heart
What transition are you facing right now?
How have your scars affected your life transitions?

Can you see the beauty in your life right now?

How can you help someone to see beauty in their life?

**Prayer**

*Father God, in faith and in hope, I say thank you.* Thank You for carrying me and sustaining me through this life. Thank You for the people whom You send to encourage me. Thank You for providing what I need when I need it. Thank You for being my joy and my strength when I have neither. Father God, sometimes this life is so hard and my scars are so painful. But I trust that You love me. I declare that You love me. You love me and my scars. I am Your letter written with the blood of Christ. May my life tell of Your goodness and Your beauty. Amen.

**Memory Verse**

> Though you have made me see troubles, many and bitter, you will restore my life again; from the depths of the earth you will again bring me up. (Psalm 71:20)

# SOME OF MY FAVORITE BIBLE VERSES

To you, O LORD, I lift my soul. I trust you, O my God. Do not let me be put to shame. Do not let my enemies triumph over me. No one who waits for you will ever be put to shame, but all who are unfaithful will be put to shame. Make your ways known to me, O LORD, and teach me your paths. Lead me in your truth and teach me because you are God, my savior. I wait all day long for you. (Psalm 25:1–5 GW)

Blessed is she who has believed that the LORD would fulfill his promises to her! (Luke 1:45)

Have I not commanded you? Be strong and courageous. Do not be afraid; do not be discouraged, for the LORD your God will be with you wherever you go. (Joshua 1:9)

Sing, barren woman, you who never bore a child; burst into song, shout for joy, you who were never in labor; because more are the children of the desolate woman than of her who has a husband, says the LORD. Enlarge the place of your tent, stretch your tent curtains wide, do not hold back; lengthen your cords, strengthen your stakes. (Isaiah 54:1–2)

But you are a chosen people, a royal priesthood, a holy nation, God's special possession, that you may declare the praises of him who called you out of darkness into His wonderful light. (1 Peter 2:9)

I am the vine; you are the branches. If you remain in me and I in you, you will bear much fruit; apart from me you can do nothing. (John 15:5)

## ABOUT THE AUTHOR

Denise Ann Goosby was born and raised in Compton, California. Her childhood love of writing led her to get an English degree from Mount St. Mary's College (now Mount St. Mary's University) and a master's degree in print journalism from the University of Southern California in Los Angeles. She later worked for the *Paramount News Tribune* newspaper, covering general and community news.

Denise has also been an educator in public and private schools for two decades. She grew up a preacher's daughter but came to faith later in life and served in several ministries in the church she was saved and discipled in.

In 2018, Denise founded Healing Song Ministries (now Ministry) to serve seniors, veterans, and the hurting in south Los Angeles County with music therapy for the heart and soul.

Denise currently writes and sings on her blog, Denise's Healing Journey at denisegoosby.com. It is there where she partners with her readers and listeners in word, song, and video to walk out our unique, God-guided paths to healing and wholeness. It is also where you may inquire about Denise's singing and speaking engagements, as well as

her proofreading, copyediting, mentoring, and one-day writing retreats for aspiring writers.

Denise enjoys spending time with friends, visiting museums and cultural sites, and cheering for her world champion childhood heroes, the Los Angeles Dodgers and Los Angeles Lakers. She is single and lives near Los Angeles.

Photo credit: Keana Clay

# CONNECT WITH DENISE

Find Denise on these social media platforms:

Facebook: https://www.facebook.com/HealingSongMinistry @ HealingSongMinistry

Facebook: Denise's Healing Journey: A Blog

YouTube: Healing Song Ministry (145) Healing Song Ministry—YouTube

LinkedIn: Twitter: @DeniseGoosby

Pinterest: @Goosbydenise

Alignable: Denise Goosby, writing, blogging, singing Your Profile (alignable.com)

Instagram: @denisegoosby

Books that are authored by or include Denise Ann Goosby:

*She Writes for Him: Stories of Living Hope*, Romans 8:28 Books, an Imprint of Redemption Press, March 2021.

*Thank You, Daddy* by Redemption Press, 2021.

Be the first to hear about new books by Denise Ann Goosby at denisegoosby.com.